MODERN BASKETBALL
FOR WOMEN

NEW DESIGNS IN
HEALTH, PHYSICAL EDUCATION AND RECREATION

Ann Paterson, *Editor*

San Francisco State College

MODERN BASKETBALL
FOR WOMEN

KENNETH D. MILLER
FLORIDA STATE UNIVERSITY

RITA JEAN HORKY
GEORGE PEABODY
COLLEGE FOR TEACHERS

Charles E. Merrill Publishing Company
A BELL & HOWELL COMPANY
COLUMBUS, OHIO

GV
886
M5

Standard Book Number: 675-09643-X

Library of Congress Catalog Card Number: 73-100638

1 2 3 4 5 6 6 8 9 10/74 73 72 71 70

PRINTED IN THE UNITED STATES OF AMERICA

PREFACE

Unfortunately, the ever-increasing interest in competitive sports for girls during recent years has not been matched by a similar increase in the training of women coaches by our professional schools of physical education.

One rather obvious reason for this situation is that most colleges offering major programs in physical education lack women faculty members who are prepared to teach the theoretical and practical aspects of sports on a varsity level. This is not meant to be a criticism of these women or of their training; it is simply a statement of fact. Generally speaking, few women physical educators working in teacher training institutions today have been exposed to the kinds of experiences needed to provide the background for adequately preparing students for coaching positions. Since the early decades of this country, there has been almost no schoolgirl athletic competition and consequently, no need to train women coaches. Now that there is a sudden demand in the public schools for such leadership, not only is there none available, but of greater concern, there is almost no faculty potential among the women professionals presently teaching in our colleges for alleviating this need in the immediate future. We are faced with a two-generation gap!

On the optimistic side of the coin is the happy indication that the controversy between the women of the AAU and the schoolwomen physical educators — the controversy which is directly responsible for the present untenable situation — is rapidly becoming past history and women, both in and out of school, who are interested in providing leadership in movement experiences for girls are beginning to work together in an effort to provide such activities at all skill levels. The cooperative rules committees, the several Olympic development programs, the National Institutes on Girls' Sports, and the gradual acceptance by the DGWS of help from men colleagues, are all concrete manifestations of this new approach.

The authors view this book as another effort in this direction. Specifically, our hope is that the provision of an up-to-date text covering the basic fundamentals of basketball will contribute toward the current need among women in athletics for a deeper understanding of the game. The material in this book has been written to serve as a reliable reference for anyone wishing to know more about basketball — the physical education student, the practicing coach, the dedicated player, or the knowledgeable fan.

Of major importance to basketball devotees in this country is the coverage of offensive and defensive team play under both the two-court and the five-player rules. As most American sportswomen know, at the 1969 annual meeting of the joint DGWS-AAU Basketball Rules Committee, it was decided that beginning with the 1969-70 playing season, women's teams would experiment with the five-player rules currently used in every country of the world *except* the United States. This progressive step obviously poses "know-how" problems for coaches and players whose only experience has been with the American two-court game, but it is the hopeful expectation of the authors that this text will contribute toward making the transition relatively painless.

Included in the coverage is the story of girls' basketball, a comprehensive analysis of the fundamental skills of the game, thorough parallel considerations of basic offensive and defensive team play under both the two-court and the five player rules, and a broad coverage of common problems facing the young coach.

The authors wish to take this opportunity of expressing their grateful appreciation to the members of the women's varsity basketball team at Midwestern College, and to the undergraduate and graduate major students at Florida State University who served so patiently as models for the photographs and diagrams used in the text.

January, 1970

                                                              K. D. M.
                                                              R. J. H.

TABLE OF CONTENTS

MODERN BASKETBALL
FOR WOMEN

CHAPTER I

A BRIEF HISTORY OF BASKETBALL FOR WOMEN IN THE UNITED STATES

IT ALL BEGAN WITH A SEMINAR

In 1891 the American physical education program consisted largely of calisthenics and other non-competitive activities such as dumbbell routines, Indian-club swinging, apparatus work, wand drills, and marching. Since most students of the time found these programs monotonous and uninteresting, physical educators and directors of non-school gymnasiums, concerned with declining motivation and falling attendance, began seeking new indoor activities to meet the needs and interests of the young people of the time.

Dr. Luther Gulick, Director of the YMCA Training School at Springfield, Massachusetts, was very much concerned with this situation since it posed a real threat to the future of the physical training phase of the work of the Y. In the fall of 1891 the problem was one presented to a group of students in a seminar in psychology conducted by Dr. Gulick at the school. Several faculty members, including James Naismith, a recently appointed instructor, were enrolled in the class. Discussions held by this group provided the springboard for Naismith's subsequent invention of the game of basketball.[1]

In seminar meetings and in informal talks with Dr. Gulick and other staff members during that fall, Naismith often had expressed the opinion that the major factor in the decline of gymnasium attendance by the young men of the day was not a dislike for activity, per se, but rather a disinterest in the traditional program. It was his belief that a new activity stressing recreation instead of physical development was

---

[1]John Dewar, "The Life and Professional Contributions of James Naismith" (unpublished Ed.D. dissertation, Florida State University, 1965), p. 38.

1

needed to rekindle zeal, and he thought that it was possible to invent a game which would accomplish this purpose.

These ideas might never have gone beyond the discussion stage had it not been that the school was faced that fall with a very concrete example of the problem. A group of prospective YMCA secretaries who were enrolled as students were most unenthusiastic about the required work in the gymnasium each day. At a faculty meeting in late November, Dr. Gulick, largely on the basis of Naismith's previous contentions, assigned this class of disgruntled scholars to him for an experimental period of two weeks.

Naismith's initial effort with the group was to have them play indoor games of low organization such as keep away, sailor's tag, and battleball, but these activities failed to alleviate the problem. As Naismith later reported, ". . . fifteen minutes of three deep became more monotonous than work on the parallel bars."[2] He next sought to develop interest in the class through variations of contemporary outdoor team sports which could be played in the gym and he introduced, in turn, adaptations of a football-rugby combination, soccer, and finally, lacrosse. These games added nothing to his objective, although they did provide ". . . a practical lesson in first aid."[3] By early December the students had not changed their views toward gymnasium activities and the experiment seemed threatened with failure.

At this point, Naismith abandoned the idea of modifying existing activities and began to study the basic principles underlying all vigorous sports — probably with the collaboration of Dr. Gulick and the other members of the seminar[4] — as a means of developing a totally new game. His first conclusion was that games invariably involve a ball, and so he began the evolution of the new activity around the concept that it, too, would be a ball game. The very nature of the indoor activity to which he was committed dictated a relatively large ball which could be handled easily and which could not be hidden. Since he did not plan to allow the ball to be carried in the new game, he decided to use a round ball, and of the various types readily available, the soccer ball was a rather obvious choice.

[2]James Naismith, *Basketball, Its Origin and Development* (New York: Association Press, 1941), p. 30.
[3]*Ibid.*, p. 40.
[4]See Marvin H. Eyler, "Origins of Some Modern Sports" (unpublished Ph.D. dissertation, University of Illinois, 1956), p. 50, in which he presents evidence that: "There are some early acquaintances of Drs. Gulick and Naismith who believe that Dr. Gulick was responsible for suggesting some of the general principles upon which this new team sport was to be based."

Naismith was seeking an indoor recreational diversion primarily for men not in training and felt that it was essential to eliminate the hazards inherent in the roughness associated with outdoor team sports of the day. He sought to accomplish this by ruling out running with the ball and the related necessity for tackling on the part of the defense. Naismith considered the elimination of roughness to be, "the fundamental principle of basketball."[5]

The idea of a horizontal goal was another attempt to minimize the jeopardy involved in the game by eliminating the driving shots characteristic of sports employing upright goals. The elevation of the goal was to prevent the massing of defensive players around the goal area. Naismith first thought of using square boxes for goals, but the closest substitution the gymnasium custodian could come up with was two peach baskets, and "baskets" have been used for goals ever since.

Obviously, Naismith's objective was to contrive a game which would not entail too much effort or too much violence, but which would provide an enjoyable recreational activity for the non-athletic YMCA secretaries–in–training with whom Dr. Gulick had challenged his ingenuity. In mid-December, 1891,[6] the new game was introduced to this group and it proved an immediate success.

The original rules were jotted down by Naismith in less than an hour on the morning of the day the game was introduced:

The ball to be an ordinary *Association* football.
1. The ball may be thrown in a direction with one or both hands.
2. The ball may be batted in a direction with one or both hands (never with the fist).
3. A player cannot run with the ball. The player must throw it from the spot on which he catches it; allowance to be made for a man who catches the ball when running at a good speed.
4. The ball must be held in or between the hands; the arms or body must not be used for holding it.
5. No shouldering, holding, pushing, tripping, or striking, in any way the person of an opponent shall be allowed; the first infringement of this rule by any person shall count as a foul, the second shall disqualify him until the next goal is made, or, if there was evident

[5]Frank G. Menke, *The New Encyclopedia of Sports* (New York: A. S. Barnes and Co., 1947), p. 179.

[6]As far as can be determined, Dr. Naismith failed to record the actual date of the first game, and, as improbable as it seems in retrospect, apparently was unable to determine it subsequently with any assurance. No specific date for this significant event in the history of sports is mentioned in any of his extant writings or addresses, nor in other available sources dealing with the history of the game.

intent to injure the person for the whole of the game, no substitute allowed.

6. A foul is striking at the ball with the fist, violation of Rules 3, 4, and such as described in Rule 5.

7. If either side makes three consecutive fouls, it shall count as a goal for the opponents. (Consecutive means without the opponents in the meantime making a foul.)

8. A goal shall be made when the ball is thrown or batted from the grounds into the basket and stays there, providing those defending the goal do not touch or disturb the goal. If the ball rests on the edge and the opponent moves the basket, it shall count as a goal.

9. When the ball goes out of bounds, it shall be thrown into the field and played by the person first touching it. In case of a dispute, the umpire shall throw it straight into the field. The thrower-in is allowed five seconds. If he holds it longer, it shall go to the opponent. If any side persists in delaying the game, the umpire shall call a foul on them.

10. The umpire shall be judge of the men and shall note the fouls and notify the referee when three consecutive fouls have been made. He shall have power to disqualify men according to Rule 5.

11. The referee shall be judge of the ball and shall decide when the ball is in play, in bounds, to which side it belongs, and shall keep time. He shall decide when a goal has been made, and keep account of the goals with any other duties that are usually performed by a referee.

12. The time shall be two fifteen minute halves, with five minutes rest between.

13. The side making the most goals in that time shall be declared the winner. In case of a draw, the game may, by agreement of the captains, be continued until another goal is made.[7]

THE WOMEN JOIN IN

Women began playing basketball when the game "was scarcely a month old,"[8] due to the coincidence that a group of young women teachers from the Buckingham Grade School happened to be passing the gym one day during the hour at which Naismith's class was scheduled. The gymnasium at the Training School was in the basement, and a door opened from the sidewalk directly into the balcony. Upon hearing the noise in the gymnasium, the teachers entered to see what was taking place and found the new game of basketball in progress. Even in its early stages basketball apparently was an exciting spectator sport and the teachers' visit to the gym became a daily occurrence.

[7]Naismith, *op. cit.,* pp. 53-55.
[8]*Ibid.,* p. 161.

Interest increased rapidly and "about two weeks after they had first come,"[9] a group of them asked Naismith why girls could not play basketball. The young instructor saw no reason why they should not, and agreed to arrange a time when the gymnasium was free for them to try the game.[10]

The women teachers appeared for this historical first practice session in their street clothes. As Naismith recalls the event:

> I shall never forget the sight that they presented in their long trailing dresses with leg-of-mutton sleeves, and in several cases with the hint of a bustle. In spite of these handicaps, the girls took the ball and began to shoot at the basket.[11]

With his typical dry humor, Dr. Naismith added: "None of the other fundamentals was observed . . ."[12]

This group organized the first girls' basketball team and practiced regularly. Gradually other teachers joined the sessions and finally enough women were participating to form two teams for intrasquad scrimmages. In March, 1892, at the conclusion of a men's tournament at the school, it was suggested that the girls have a contest. Another team was organized among a group of stenographers and faculty wives, and the first scheduled competition in women's basketball was held at this time.

From Springfield the game spread rapidly as the new sport found quick recognition among directors of physical training in the women's colleges. Although Senda Berenson, the director of physical training at Smith College, reported that basketball was being played at that institution as early as 1892[13], Naismith states that Miss Berenson first became interested in basketball at a physical education convention held at Yale in 1893, where he told her that girls were playing the game in Springfield. According to Naismith, "Miss Berenson spent some time studying basketball in order that she might introduce it at Smith."[14] We do know that in 1893, a contest was played at Smith between the freshman and sophomore teams. The press reports of this

---

[9]*Ibid.*
[10]The several vague references to the date of this first playing of the game by women indicate that it was probably in either late January or early February of 1892.
[11]Naismith, *op. cit.,* p. 162.
[12]*Ibid.*
[13]Senda Berenson (ed.), *Line Basket Ball or Basket Ball for Women* (New York: American Sports Publishing Co., 1901), p. 5.
[14]Naismith, *op. cit.,* p. 163.

match included the observation: "No men were allowed as the young ladies wore bloomers."[15]

Within the next few years the popularity of the game increased throughout the United States. During this early growth, Clara Baer of New Orleans' Sophie Newcomb College began experimenting with the game and in 1895 published a set of rules for what she called "Basquette." Among other variations from the men's game was the division of the playing court into three areas. According to Naismith, this was not intended by Miss Baer to be a change from the men's rules. The 1893 *Second Edition of the Rules Book* for men had included a diagram indicating the general floor positions of the nine players, which separated the forwards, the centers, and the backs by two dotted lines running across the diagram and dividing the court playing area into thirds. Miss Baer interpreted these as being restraining lines,[16] and the three-court game was thus established as the official pattern of basketball for women for the next 43 years!

The first called meeting to discuss feasible rules for girls convened in 1898. Feeling that the boys' game was too strenuous for women and that certain modifications of the published rules were desirable, this first "rules committee" for the women's game suggested the following changes:

1. The ball could not be taken away from the player who was holding it.
2. The player in possession of the ball could not hold it longer than three seconds.
3. The floor was divided into three sections, and a player could not cross these lines under penalty of a foul.
4. A defending player could not reach over another player who was in possession of the ball. The arms must be kept in a verticolateral plane, and a violation of this rule by a defensive player was called overguarding.[17]

Other schools and other localities were also unilaterally drawing up girls' rules during this period, and before the game was out of its infancy there were few sections of the country playing basketball alike. Thus it was quite natural that at a physical training conference held at Springfield from June 14 to June 28, 1899, a committee was appointed to study the situation and to draw up a standard set of rules for girls.

---

[15]Lamont Buchanan, *The Story of Basketball* (New York: Stephen-Paul Publishers, 1948), pp. 62-63.
[16]Naismith, *op. cit.,* pp. 165-66.
[17]*Ibid.,* p. 166.

The chairman of this historically important group was Dr. Alice Foster, M.D., Director of Physical Training for Women at Oberlin College. The other members of the committee ware Ethel Perrin, Boston Normal School of Gymnastics; Elizabeth Wright, Radcliffe College; and Senda Berenson, Smith College. The report of this committee and the rules which it proposed were adopted unanimously by the conference.

The chief changes made by the committee in adapting the men's rules in effect at the time for play by women were similar to those recommended by the New York group the previous year: (1) the division of the playing court into three equal areas; (2) a rule against "snatching or batting" the ball from the hands of an opposing player; (3) the introduction of the three-bounce dribble; (4) a three-second limit on holding the ball; and, (5) the establishment of the number of players on a team as being not less than five nor more than ten.

Naismith's original idea concerning the number of players on a side, incidentally, was simply that the game should accommodate whatever number of students were in his class. The nine-man team represented no magic figure. Since there were eighteen men in his historic group of YMCA secretaries-in-training, the first game was played with nine men on each side — three forwards, three centers, and three backs. For several years thereafter the normal procedure in organizing a game was to divide a group into two teams, regardless of the number involved, and let them play.[18] This often proved somewhat hectic and with his Scotch tongue in cheek, Naismith reported an early experience of Edward Hitchcock, Jr., the Physical Director at Cornell, who utilized this concept in introducing the game to a class of 100 men at Ithaca:

> On the second day, Hitchcock decided that this plan would not do, as there was grave danger of serious damage to the building. He decided that fifty men on a side were too many for basketball.[19]

BASKETBALL — A GIRLS' GAME

It is quite evident that Dr. Naismith originally had no idea that his game would ever be played by girls, but by the turn of the century it was firmly established as the most popular sports activity participated in by American women. Dorothy Ainsworth tells us that basketball was mentioned in catalogs and other school publications before 1900 at such well-regarded women's colleges as Barnard, Bryn Mawr, Elmira,

---

[18]*Ibid.,* p. 72.
[19]*Ibid.,* p. 73.

Goucher, Mills, Mt. Holyoke, Radcliffe, Rockford, Smith, Vassar, Wellesley, and Wells;[20] and by 1903, Ellen Bernard Thompson wrote:

Today, all the important colleges for women . . . are represented by regular basket-ball teams, and most of the larger institutions have adopted basket-ball as a factor in physical training.[21]

Because of its rapid acceptance by women, and because of the deliberate intent of the early rules makers to eliminate body contact from the game, basketball, by the second decade of its development, was well on its way toward becoming primarily a girls' sport. Although the game was promoted enthusiastically at YMCA gymnasiums, it was widely considered a rather effeminate pastime for men and boys.

This opinion was world-wide wherever the game was known. Basketball was introduced to English girls by Bessie Fotheringham soon after its origin. Its immediate acceptance typed the game as a girls' sport and English men refused to play until recent years. On the other side of the world where basketball was already an important part of the physical education program for Japanese women by 1900, it was not accepted as a men's sport until about 1913.[22] In the Philippine Islands, too, the game was first played by girls, and not until American men and boys set the example did Filipino men take up the sport.[23] In 1907 basketball was introduced into New Zealand as a girls' outdoor sport by the Rev. J. C. Jamieson who had seen the game played by women in Australia. This variation, "outdoor" basketball, is still played exclusively by girls and women down under, although men began playing "indoor" basketball in the late 1920s in the YMCA's, and this interest was accentuated through overseas contacts during World War II. Women's indoor basketball is a comparatively new sport first played competitively in 1946.[24] Basketball was played by girls in Brazil as early as 1896 and in some sections of South America, including parts of Brazil, the game was still considered a girls' sport as late as the early 1940s.[25]

It is an interesting observation of human nature that despite the rather general concept in the early days of the game that basketball

[20]Dorothy S. Ainsworth, *The History of Physical Education in Colleges for Women* (New York: A. S. Barnes and Co., 1930), pp. 29-30.

[21]Lucille Eaton Hill (ed.), *Athletics and Out-Door Sports for Women.* Ch. 12, "Basket-Ball" by Ella Bernard Thompson (New York: The Macmillan Co., 1903), p. 241.

[22]Naismith, *op. cit.,* p. 152.

[23]Menke, *op. cit.,* p.183.

[24]Information from the New Zealand Embassy, Washington, D. C., April 5, 1968.

[25]Naismith, *op. cit.,* p. 150.

was a "sissy game," girls who played at this time usually ran the risk of being regarded as "tomboys"! Such stereotyping didn't seem to impede the interest of girls, however, and women physical educators recognized its potential as a valuable addition to the school program from the beginning. Berenson voiced the opinion of most when she wrote "Women have long felt the need of some sport that would combine both the physical development of gymnastics and the abandon and delight of true play."[26] Although such comments were widely expressed, not all sports leaders accepted the game without reservation. The early concern over the rules indicates that some women looked with disapproval upon the aggressiveness inherent in the competitive elements of the sport. A few prominent physical educators were outspoken in their objections. In 1903, a *New York Times* news item reported that Lucille Eaton Hill, Director of Physical Training at Wellesley College, ". . . startled the New England Association of Colleges and Preparatory Schools by a spirited attack on basketball."[27] The article quoted her as saying:

> Basketball, . . . should be stopped absolutely so far as girls under the college age is concerned, and it should be admitted only tentatively, and under professional supervision, to a place among the sports open to women of a new age . . . the chances of permanent injury to beauty and health, the evil influence of such excitement upon the emotional and nervous feminine nature, and the tendency to unsex the player — for she declared that the competitive game, with its traveling about, its exhibitions before mixed audiences, and its cultivation of the win-at-any-cost spirit, was not womanly, and made neither for character nor refinement — were all urged against the game for young girls.[28]

NATIONAL CHAMPS!

National scholastic championships in girls' basketball were determined over a three-year span from 1924 through 1926. The first national title was won by the Guthrie (Oklahoma) High School team which represented the West in an intersectional championship playoff against the Westfield (New Jersey) High School girls, the Eastern champions. Guthrie defeated Westfield 32-22 and 34-17 in a best-of-three series held at Westfield in April of 1924.

In April of 1925 four high school teams competed for the national scholastic title at Hempstead, New York. The championship was won

---

[26]Senda Berenson, "Basket Ball for Women," *Physical Education,* III (September, 1894), p. 106.
[27]*New York Times,* October 11, 1903, Part 2, p. 11.
[28]*Ibid.*

by the Hempstead High School squad which defeated Burlington (Vermont) High School in the first round and Struthers High School of Youngstown, Ohio, in the finals.

The 1926 tournament was held at Youngstown in March. The national title was won by the girls from Sharon (Pennsylvania) High School who won over the home town Struthers High School in the championship game.

The first National AAU championship tournament for women was held in 1926 at Pasadena, California, and the winner of the initial title was the team representing the Pasadena Athletic and Country Club. Schepp's Aces, a Dallas team, won the second National AAU tournament, held at Wichita, Kansas in 1929. This year saw the selection of the first AAU women's All America team composed of Louise Milam and Gypsy Williams of the championship Schepp's Aces squad; Agnes Iori and Verna Montgomery of the Dallas Golden

FIGURE 1-1   Nera White demonstrates faultless jump shot technique at the 1968 NAAU Championships.

Cyclone; Thelma Russell of the Cisco (Texas) Kittens; and Quinnie Hamm of the Sparkman (Arkansas) Sparklers.

Since the second tournament, national championships have been staged annually. In recent years the Nashville Business College has dominated the competition, winning the title eleven times between 1950 and 1969. Among the many fine athletes who contributed to this long rule by the Nashville club, two players, Nera White and Joan Crawford, must be singled out as being among the most extraordinary performers in the history of women's sports.

Nera White was first selected as an All-American in 1955 and through 1969 she had been chosen for this honor fifteen consecutive times! Miss White obviously qualifies as one of the most durable top flight athletes of record and her being voted the "Most Valuable Player" in the 1969 National AAU Tournament — fourteen years after first being chosen for the All-American team — is almost inconceivable.

The longevity of this remarkable athlete's maintenance of national-class performance was closely paralleled by a Nashville teammate, Joan Crawford, who like Miss White, is a charter member of the Helms Women's Basketball Hall of Fame. From 1957 through 1969 Miss Crawford was named to thirteen consecutive All America squads, while playing for the Clarendon (Texas) Junior College and the Nashville Business College teams.

A third athlete who ranked as one of the country's best for over a decade was Alline Banks Sprouse, an eleven–time All-American selection between 1940 and 1950, while playing for several different teams (the Nashville Business College, the Vultee Convacs, the Nashville Gold-blumes, and the Atlanta Blues).

THE GREAT CONTROVERSY

In spite of early attempts to standardize the rules, from the turn of the century until the present the game has been played under a some-times bewildering variety of regulations. Variations have existed on the national, regional, state, and even local levels! Much of the responsi-bility for the prolongation of this unfortunate situation must be laid at the feet of the two women's groups whose different sets of rules have been most widely used over the years — the Amateur Athletic Union, and the Division for Girls' and Women's Sports (and its predecessors, the NSGWS and the NSWA) of the American Association for Health, Physical Education, and Recreation. For forty–some years, beginning in 1922 shortly after the AAU officially asserted its authority over all open competition in athletic events conducted for women, these two organizations conducted a continuing feud based primarily upon professional jealousies, although both groups rationalized the cause as being one of "philosophical differences." Whatever the reasons, the result not only prevented any practical consideration of rules standardization, but of much greater consequence, severely curtailed the overall sports participation of several generations of American girls.

The alleged basis of this most unfortunate controversy was the opinion of women physical educators to the effect that the AAU promoted sports for girls with little concern for standards related to the welfare of the participants. This conviction led, somewhat illogically, to an unbending stand against the participation of schoolgirls in any high-level competitive sports and to an inevitable decline of such programs in schools and colleges.

During these years, women of the AAU were determined to make no concessions to what they considered impractical and petty restrictions, and their reaction to the physical educators was simply to ignore them and their school-oriented programs. This policy, of course, only increased the scope of the eclipse of interscholastic sports for girls—programs which were (and still are) the only solution for the problem of providing the essential training pools for the AAU's efforts to upgrade performance standards of American women athletes.

Basketball continued to thrive, however, in spite of the virtual elimination of high-level competition for schoolgirls resulting from this quarrel. It was already the most widely played team sport for girls before the controversy developed and its popularity continued to increase throughout the period of stalemate between the women leaders of the two opposing factions. Nevertheless, this long-delayed meeting of minds cannot be viewed in retrospect as anything but an irretrievable backward step in the development of women's competitive sports, in general, and of girls' basketball, in particular.

During the 1955-65 decade, there was a gradual reconciliation of the differences between the AAU and the DGWS as women on both sides of the issue increasingly became aware of the probability that they had been more concerned with maintaining a position than with acting in the best interests of girls.

Two aspects of the this long-overdue meeting of minds were especially significant. First, the AAU gradually conceded that the standards of the physical educators were acceptable and worthy goals for *all* women in competitive sports. Paralleling this slowly evolving concept, the DGWS finally began to accept the fact that competitive athletics for women were a vital and worthwhile part of the culture pattern of most of the civilized world, and that sports programs for girl athletes were as important as such programs for girl non-athletes.

One of the first benefits of this painfully arrived at mutual understanding was the 1958 meeting of the Basketball Rules Committee of the DGWS and representatives of the AAU to consider standardization of the rules then in use by the two groups. Between 1958 and 1964, these two organizations continued to meet together for this purpose and both adopted modifications periodically which gradually eliminated the differences between the two sets of rules. By the 1964-65 season, they were identical. Shortly thereafter, an operating code for a joint rules committee was developed. This provided for a committee of six members from the DGWS and six from the AAU, with the chairmanship to be rotated annually between the two groups. This significant forward step in the progress of women's basketball was implemented on January 1, 1968, when the Joint DGWS-AAU Basketball Rules Committee was officially authorized to begin its tenure.

INTERNATIONAL COMPETITION

The first appearance of a women's basketball team representing the United States in international competition was in a four-game series held in Cleveland and Brooklyn in April of 1926, between the Newman-Stern girls' team from Cleveland, and the Edmonton Grads — a team made up of graduates from McDougall Commercial High School in Edmonton, Alberta, Canada. This series was billed as a match for the "world's championship" — a title which the Grads had claimed since 1922 — and was decided on a total point basis for four games. The U. S. team captured the series with a total score of 73-60 while winning three games of the four played.

From this period until the World War II years, international competition for women's teams from the United States was limited to games with the famed Edmonton team. Most of these matches were played in best-of-five series and although American teams won some games, with the exception of one set-back in 1933, the Canadian girls were able to defend their claim to the "International Women's Basketball Championship" with monotonous regularity. The 1933 reversal was at the hands of the Durante (Oklahoma) Cardinals, who won the national AAU title that year, as well as beating the Grads three-straight for the world crown. Two years later, the Edmonton team reassumed the women's world championship by defeating the 1935 U. S. national champions, the Tulsa Stenos, three games out of four in a challenge series.

The Fourth Women's World Games were held in London in 1934 and the sole representative of the United States was the girls' basketball team from Oklahoma City University, runner-up in the 1934 AAU tournament. This was our first venture into international basketball competition abroad, and it was, unfortunately, not a winning one. The Americans were defeated for the title by the French team in what apparently was one of the most farcical international sports matches of all time.[29] The single referee was a compatriot of the French team, costumed, according to news reports, as a Swiss yodeler, complete with mountaineer boots, knee-length stockings, hiking shorts, and a Tyrolean cap topped with feather! This official would not allow the players to pivot or dribble and they were not permitted to speak while play was in progress.

The game was held out-of-doors at the White City Stadium in conjunction with the track and field competition, and play was stopped when any of these events were in progress. Neither team was allowed to substitute and all of the one-way communication with the American team was conducted in a violent sign language. Coral Warley was the outstanding U. S. player with eight points, but as the *New York Times* reported, ". . . when the match was all over . . . [the referee] alone apparently had any idea of what it was all about."[30]

From the beginnings of World War II in the mid-1930's through the 1940's, international basketball for women was shelved. During the war years the game was limited largely to the various military services, and in the immediate post-war era, foreign powers were pointing their efforts in women's sports toward track and field, swimming, and gymnastics because of the political implications involved in Olympic competition. As soon as such programs were well established, however, those nations underwriting the popular world-wide game of making the United States look bad, turned to the team sports arena. Basketball, invented by the Americans, was obviously a logical (and vulnerable) first priority target for these countries in their expanding developmental efforts in athletics for women.

The First World Championship Tournament for Women was held in 1953, at Santiago, and was won by the United States team which defeated Chile 49-36 in the final round. Pauline Bowden was the key player for our girls, scoring 22 points in the title game.

In 1955, basketball for women was included for the first time as a regular event in the Second Pan American Games held in Mexico City. The United States entered a team which won the championship by sweeping through the double round robin tournament undefeated. Lurlyne Greer Mealhouse, later a charter member of the Helms Hall

---

[29]*New York Times,* August 12, 1934, sec. 3, p. 1.
[30]*Ibid.*

of Fame, was the outstanding U. S. Player, scoring 140 points in eight games for a 17.5 average. Chile and Brazil finished second and third in the team standings, and there were clear-cut indications that the game of basketball was being taken very seriously indeed by women outside the United States.

Two years later at Rio de Janeiro, the American girls captured the Women's World Championship title for the second consecutive time by defeating the Russians 51-48 before 40,000 fans! Barbara Sipes of Iowa Wesleyan College was the leading U. S. scorer in the championship game with 18 points, and Nera White was named the tournament's "Most Valuable Player."

In April of 1958 a team composed largely of players from the Nashville Business College, AAU Champions of that year, toured the Soviet Union, winning four out of six contests. Barbara Sipes, Sandra Fiete, and Nera White were the outstanding players for the American team. Both losses were to the Soviet national team in Moscow. The wins were at the expense of more lightly regarded Russian squads at Tiflis and Leningrad.

Chicago was the host city for the third staging of the Pan American Games in 1959. The American team again won the basketball crown with eight straight wins, but it was obvious that never again would we merely have to put in an appearance to pick up the gold medals. Chile despite double losses to both the United States and Brazil, produced the two leading scorers in the tournament — Irene Velasquez, with 147 points, and Ismenia Pouchard, with 114 points. Rita Horky, who led the U. S. scorers with 95 points, and Joan Crawford were the outstanding U. S. players.

After the Chicago Games, Harley Redin, Wayland Baptist College Coach, who doubled as Coach of the American team in the Games, sounded a warning of dark days ahead, and suggested the need for longer training periods and more play under international rules. But hardly anyone listened; wasn't basketball "our" game?

The Russians Are Coming!

In the late fall of 1959 the Soviet Union returned the visit of the United States team to Russia the previous year and defeated our top teams, the Nashville Business College, Wayland Baptist College, and Iowa Wesleyan College, in six straight games.

The Americans, in turn, sent a national team to Russia in 1961, and split eight games against various Soviet teams in Moscow, Tiflis, Kiev, and Leningrad. Despite fine performances by Joan Crawford in the two Moscow games, the Russian national team handily beat the Americans in these key contests, 65-48 and 55-45.

Russia repaid this visit in 1962, and their European championship team repeated their sweep of 1959, winning eight straight games against the Nashville Business College, Iowa Wesleyan College, and Wayland College. Although the first contest against NBC was a double–overtime thriller, the awesome Russian team ran up 103 points in one of the Iowa Wesleyan games.

The Fourth Pan American Games were held at São Paulo in 1963, and although the United States girls won the team championship for the third straight time, the U. S. team and the Brazilians split their two games in the double round robin (Brazil's win, incidentally, was before some 30,000 partisan *aficionados*) and ended the regular tourney play with identical 7-1 records. Again, as at Chicago four years previously, the two Nashville Business College teammates, Joan Crawford and Rita Horky, were standouts for the U. S. Miss Crawford had 22 points in the crucial playoff game, and Miss Horky proved her world-class, two-way ability by being singled out this time as the defensive star of the tournament.

The 1964 Women's World Championships were held at Lima. The U. S. team finished fourth behind the Soviet Union, Czechoslovakia, and Bulgaria. Despite the poor finish of our team, Rita Horky capped her career by being chosen for the "All-World" team.

Two years later the Soviets returned to the United States, and won six straight games against our best teams. The closest any U. S. team could come to the Russians was a 50-35 loss suffered by the Nashville Business College.

A momentary bright spot surrounding the basketball picture in the mid-1960s, was the institution, in 1966, of the Helms Women's Basketball Hall of Fame, honoring sixteen of the outstanding players in the history of AAU competition. The charter members as cited included:

Alline Banks	Corine Jaax
Leota Barham	Evelyn Jordan
Loretta Blann	Mary Marshall
Alberta Lee Cox	Margaret Sexton
Joan Crawford	Lucille Thurman
Lurlyne Greer	Hazel Walker
Mary Winslow Hoffay	Nera White
Rita Horky	Alberta Williams

For three weeks in March and April of 1967, just prior to the Fifth Women's World Championships, a basketball training camp was held at Blue Eye, Missouri, for the specific purpose of preparing our team for the international competition ahead.

That such a program was too little and too late was evident in the results of the Tournament held in Czechoslovakia immediately following the camp. Despite the serious pre-tourney preparation and a squad which included five All-Americans, our girls returned from Europe with the poorest record to date of any United States women's basketball team in an international tournament. No one at home was surprised

FIGURE 1-2   Rita Horky defends against Bulgarian player at the 1964 World Championships held in Lima, Peru. Miss Horky was selected on the All-World team at the conclusion of this tournament.

at the ability of the Russians — we knew about them! — but the fact that South Korea, Czechoslovakia, Japan, and East Germany all fielded teams of the same class was a rude shock. In Czechoslovakia our team lost to the Russians, the Yugoslavians, the Italians, the Brazilians, and the Bulgarians, while compiling a 1-6 tournament record. Among the unbelievable (to Americans, that is) happenings of this eye-opening European trip, was the selection of Park Shin-Ja, *a member of the Korean team,* as the tournament's "Most Valuable Player"!

Later in 1967, at Winnipeg, the Brazilian women underlined the obvious fact that our national effort in promoting women's basketball was inadequate, by winning the championship at the Fifth Pan American Games with an unblemished eight straight victories, including two over the United States team.

Lessons From History

While it is difficult to find anything for Americans to be enthusiastic about in the 20-0 win-loss record compiled by the Soviet teams in their 1959, 1962, and 1966 tours of the United States, the visits were in one way beneficial. After the 1962 debacle, it finally became evident to even the most persistent die-hards, that the American game in its intramural setting would no longer provide adequate preparation for the development of the calibre of basketball needed to participate successfully in world-class competition, and in December of 1962, a long-range plan to upgrade the athletic performance level of American girls through a series of national workshops was recommended by the Women's Board of the U. S. Olympic Committee. Under the direction of U. S. Olympic Development Committee and the AAHPER, this concept evolved into the National Institutes on Girls' Sports which were made possible through a grant from the Doris Duke Foundation. The first Institute was held at the University of Oklahoma in 1963, and since that date additional workshops have been scheduled at various locations throughout the country. Basketball has been included frequently in these programs.

Three significant factors were involved in this effort: (1) a beginning was finally made toward meeting some of the needs and interests of those American schoolgirls endowed with superior athletic potential; (2) this action was another indication of the new spirit of cooperation between school-oriented and non-school groups of women in athletics in which the welfare of girls was put above petty organizational rivalries; and (3) at last, the necessity of doing something about the less than spectacular success of American women in international athletic competition was recognized — a factor which, in world politics since World War II, has had implications vital to our national interest. The 1966 visit of the grim and determined Russian team was again, as after their previous tour of America, followed almost immediately by action aimed at improving the performance of our young players. 1967 saw the inauguration of a six-year development program by the AAU Women's Basketball Committee and the United States Olympic Basketball Committee, consisting of a series of yearly training camps to be rotated through different sections of the country each year through 1972. The record of our team in the 1967 Czechoslovakian world tourney indicated that a program of this nature was long overdue, and that it was, at best, barely a minimum essential.

The obvious implication of the 1960s was that not only the Soviet Union, but also many other parts of the world were giving a great deal of attention to the preparation of women basketball players (and other women athletes, too!) for international competition. The fact that in some countries this was outright exploitation of athletes for purely political purposes is beside the point. Women, the world over, were becoming increasingly sports-minded, and if the United States planned to compete in basketball on even terms with foreign teams, widely increased opportunities would have to be found for our athletes at all ages and skills levels to play under international rules, and for our national teams to play against world-class competition more frequently.

FIGURE 1-3   United States squad at the First Olympic Development Camp, Blue Eye, Missouri, 1967.

The training camp concept of the Olympic Committee was a step in the right direction. Something had to be done to give our teams an opportunity to practice together prior to entering tournaments in which they would compete against highly trained women's squads from an increasing number of foreign powers. Periodic three-week periods of training and conditioning, however, did not and will not provide a solution to the problem of keeping up with the Russians (or even the South Koreans). The National Institutes on Girls' Sports with their emphasis on the upgrading of coaching know-how among women physical educators, has been a move with tremendously greater potential significance. These institutes, the concomitant trend toward ever-increasing opportunities for athletic competition among American schoolgirls, and the experimental adoption by the joint rules committee of the five-player team concept — the basic principle of international rules — were the important developments of the revolutionary decade of the 1960s. Such a positive trend, if continued, cannot help but pay handsome dividends in the future.

CHAPTER II

CONDITIONING

There are two closely related aspects of a training program for girls preparing for a season of competitive basketball. The most obvious, perhaps, is that the individuals making up the team must learn to perform the fundamental motor skills of the game with at least some degree of adequacy. The other, more basic, aspect is that these girls must be conditioned physically and mentally for the stresses and strains of the playing season. These two features, the development of skill and the improvement of fitness, are essential elements of any athletic training program, and most of the standard procedures used by basketball coaches are designed to contribute toward both of these aspects. Although interdependent, the two objectives do have different connotations, and the content of this chapter deals briefly with the "conditioning" of the girl player.

As basketball for girls gradually has evolved into the modern game, it has become increasingly a sport characterized by almost continuous running. This means that before a girl is ready to perform adequately in the modern-day game, she must have attained a high state of physical fitness. She must "get in shape." She must be *conditioned*.

To the coach, the term conditioning refers to a procedure aimed at bringing about an increase in physical and psychological readiness through the regulation of the athlete's *exercise, rest,* and *nutrition.* The extent to which the coach understands the principles underlying the complex interrelationships between these factors, and the degree of sacrifice that the girl is willing to make in cooperation with his suggestions in this regard, will determine the measure of improvement in the athlete's fitness.

EXERCISE

The importance of exercise to physical fitness is well understood by physiologists. Man is a muscular organism and muscles require movement in order to acquire and maintain optimum efficiency and effectiveness. Because of his very nature, exercise is a *need* of man, and the attainment of a desirable state of physical fitness is impossible without regular, vigorous big-muscle activity. On a less basic level, the coach is concerned with exercise in its relationshp to such specific factors of fitness as strength, endurance, agility, and flexibility, since these are the aspects of the fitness concept toward which exercise can make a significant contribution.

Strength

Motor performance is dependent upon many complex influences, but basic to sports potential is the factor known as *power*. Power is the product of strength and speed of muscle contraction and, obviously, it would be to any would-be athlete's advantage to attempt to increase these two components. Unfortunately, not much can be done about the speed of one's muscular contraction after conception. This factor is an innate characteristic. Strength, however, is a physical quality which can be improved readily by the typical girl athlete if she is motivated to do so. An increase in strength will improve any girl's performance level, but the only way to achieve such an increase is through hard work. It is a readily observed fact that muscular development is dependent upon the demand made on the muscles. Blacksmiths are robust and strong; office clerks are often scrawny (or overweight) and weak. This is visible evidence of the overload principle in action. Strength is augmented by increasing the normal work load applied to a muscle. There is no easy way to improve strength. It takes work, but the resulting improvement in performance is, for the dedicated athlete, worth the price.

With an increase in strength there is a growth in muscle girth due to a multiplication in the number of capillaries, an accretion in the amount of connective tissue, and an enlargement of existing muscle fibers. Because of this fact, many girls tend to avoid strengthening exercises from the misconception that such activities will result in the development of a musculature considered masculine. The truth of the matter is that vigorous participation in athletics will not change a girl's physique from that with which she was endowed by nature — hereditary factors in the genes control this outcome. Such bodily changes that do occur from strength-building exercises will be assets to any girl's figure rather than detriments — whatever body type she was lucky or unlucky enough to inherit!

Endurance

Endurance is another trait basic to the concept of physical fitness. It can be defined as the ability of a muscle to perform continuous work over an extended period of time and, like strength, it is improved through the application of the overload principle. Endurance is developed by increasing the number of contractions made by a muscle under a sustained load, and thus, the emphasis of endurance exercises is upon repetition rather than upon the resistance to which a muscle or muscle group is subjected.

An increase in endurance results from physiological modifications — primarily an increased capillarization in the muscle tissue which provides a greater volume of blood supply and an improvement in the mechanical efficiency of the entire cardiovascular system in supplying oxygen and in removing the waste products of metabolism.

OFF-SEASON TRAINING

In terms of the normal competitive season, basketball is a winter sport and the training program usually begins in the fall semester shortly after the opening of school. The conditioning program of the girl athlete, however, should not be limited to the period of the basketball season. Training, for those who have serious intentions concerning the development of their athletic potential is, by necessity, a year-around operation. Even for the girl with a more casual objective in sports, conditioning should be thought of as a long-term process. The physiological advantages inherent in gradual conditioning are well documented and crash programs — which unfortunately are the common pattern of conditioning found in most American schools — are not in the best interests of any competitor.

While a year-around program is important for the general well-being of the girl athlete, the off-season participation should be devoted to activities other than basketball and preferably at a less intensive level of effort than that put forth during the winter playing season. Regular participation several days per week, in tennis, swimming, or any other demanding sports activity, plus a jogging program, will provide the exercise needed to maintain a desirable level of strength and cardio-

vascular efficiency through the summer. The change of pace recommended in the shift to a different sport will help to bring the girl to
the first basketball turn-out mentally refreshed and eager to get the
new season underway.

Jogging

For many reasons, jogging is an ideal exercise not only during the
off-season of the girl athlete, but as a life-long habit pattern for the
typical man and woman. Running is one of the so-called "natural"
or "racial" movements of man and no matter how inept one may be
in terms of motor skill, anyone without a handicapping anomaly can
run with at least some degree of effectiveness.* Jogging is an activity
in which one can participate alone or in a group, and without specialized
facilities or equipment. People can and do run everywhere — on the
beach sand, across golf links, through school and college campuses,
over open fields, in the parks or woods, and even through the streets
in urban residential areas — at any hour of the day or night. Possibly
the strongest point in favor of jogging as a conditioning exercise is
the adaptability of the activity to the specific needs of the individual
through modifications in pace, distance covered, or time expended.

PRE-SEASON TRAINING

Four to six weeks prior to the beginning of the formal basketball
practice season candidates for the team should begin a serious conditioning program stressing exercises designed to increase strength,
endurance, and agility. This suggestion implies a shift in emphasis
from the maintenance–type effort of the summer to a strenuous overload program in final preparation for the playing season. As a prelude
to the initiation of this program, each candidate for the team should
receive a thorough physical examination. This check-up *prior* to the
beginning of the formal training phase of the basketball season is an
indispensable feature of any sound sports program.

As previously indicated, there is no easy road to the development
of either strength or endurance. These characteristics are increased only
through hard work, and the smart coach will vary the activities in order
to keep the interest of the athlete from lagging. A medley of exercise
patterns should be utilized, including weight training, *fartlek,* interval
training, and circuit training.

---

*See pages 63-66 for a consideration of the mechanics of running.

Weight Training

It is an unfortunate fact that many people still confuse weight training with the activity from which it evolved, weight lifting. In spite of the similarity in names and in the equipment used the two activities serve completely different purposes. Weight lifting is a man's competitive sport in which the objective is to lift a maximum weight to an extended position over the head by the use of three specific lifting techniques. Weight training, on the other hand, is an exercise program based upon resistance to a graded overload, being used increasingly by both men and women as a means of improving fitness or performance ability. Such a program improves the physical components which contribute toward a girl's general fitness, sports ability, and overall attractiveness. At the present time, top-flight women athletes throughout the world almost without exception, include weight training in some phase of their conditioning.

Weight training is a program in which a pre-established number of repetitions (called a set) of a prescribed resistance exercise[1] are gradually increased over a period of time until a fixed number has been reached. At this point additional weight is added to the exercise, the number of repetitions in each set reverts to the starting number, and the pattern is repeated.

Fartlek

Fartlek is a Swedish training and conditioning activity which has gained enthusiastic acceptance with coaches and athletes the world over. The term *fartlek* is roughly translated as "speed play," an expression which describes the concept with considerable precision. The activity consists of jogging interspersed by brief, all-out sprints and by periods of fast striding. The "play" concept of this training lies in the fact that the pace variation is changed at the will of the runner. *Fartlek* is ideally adapted to open country running, but the pattern can be followed just as well on any running course.

Although the first few days of *fartlek* training should mix the three running paces without undue strain on the participant, in order for the activity to be effective as a means of increasing fitness, the sprinting and

---

[1]For a further consideration of weight training, including suggested exercises, see: Kenneth D. Miller, *Track and Field for Girls* (New York: Ronald Press Company, 1964), pp. 19-21; and Kenneth D. Miller (ed.), *Physical Education Activities for College Men and Women* (Dubuque, Iowa: Wm. C. Brown Company, (1963), pp. 50-52.

striding phases must be run at a demanding level. Calling an endurance exercise "play" doesn't change the fact that only hard, purposeful work — an overload — will produce the sought after physiological adaptations.

Fartlek is especially useful as an early pre-season training technique because of the responsibility for self-discipline imposed upon each girl. This is an essential trait for any athlete to acquire and in this kind of program the opportunities inherent for the coach to plan the day's work with each girl before every practice session, and to evaluate it after the workout, are important in developing the effective pupil-teacher relationship which is the basis of successful coaching.

Interval Training

Interval training is an endurance building program in which strenuous work for a given period of time is alternated with a recovery period. This procedure is repeated a number of times depending upon the condition of the participant. As the athlete's endurance improves, the pace at which the exercise is performed can be intensified, the length of the recovery phase can be shortened, or the number of repetitions can be increased. Intensive training patterns can be established in running, swimming, calisthenic exercises, or any other vigorous activity. For basketball players, however, running is the recommended stress to use during the pre-season training period.

A recommended beginning stress-recovery-stress sequence for a girl basketball player is a constant-pace jog of 220 yards in 60 seconds, followed by a 220-yard walk. This design is continued for six to eight repetitions, and with typical girl athletes, the pace and/or the distance can be increased after the first three days of such training.

The length of the recovery period in interval training patterns should be determined on the basis of how the individual runner feels. Each girl should start every repetition with both heart rate and respiration near normal. The runner in an interval training program must be fresh enough at the beginning of each repetition to maintain the pre-established pace.

Circuit Training

Circuit training is a program in which a series of specific exercises are performed in sequence at numbered stations. The athlete moves as rapidly as possible from one station to another performing the prescribed exercise at each stop. The time required to complete the initial circuit is recorded and this becomes the target criterion which the girl attempts to better on succeeding trials. One obvious motivating agent in this form of conditioning is the fact that each individual competes against herself and is therefore able to progress at her own rate of development.

Normally, each station features a different type of exercise consisting of strengthening, muscle endurance, agility, cardiovascular endurance, or flexibility. The circuit training concept includes an emphasis on continuous motion and the girls are encouraged to jog (or run!) between stations in order to maintain activity from the starting point until the end. Prolonged rhythmic action is a primary factor in the development of cardiovascular fitness and the challenge of beating the circuit is deliberately aimed at promoting such effort.

As a girl's condition improves, the stress may be increased by adding laps of the same circuit, by increasing the number of repetitions of the exercises at each station, by adding stations, or by lowering the target time in which to complete the sequence.

NUTRITION

Earlier in this chapter it was pointed out that a successful physical conditioning program must be based upon three primary factors — adequate exercise, adequate rest, and adequate nutrition. The latter component, nutrition, refers to the sum of the processes by which the body utilizes food substances, and adequate nutrition obviously implies a condition in which the body is supplied with the nourishment essential to meeting the demands made upon it. Competitive basketball makes extraordinary demands upon the body and since the food taken in is the only source of fuel for energy, building materials for the repair and growth of tissues, and regulators for the control of body functions, the adequacy of each girl's nutrition must be of particular concern to the coach in her effort to increase the level of physical fitness among the candidates for the team.

Foods

Food products are classified as carbohydrates, fats, and proteins. Since each of these substances is present in all living cells, each is an essential component of the adequate diet. Other indispensable dietary elements include certain inorganic salts (usually referred to simply as minerals), water, and a number of complex organic compounds called vitamins.

Carbohydrates compose a relatively large proportion of the energy-yielding materials in foods. They are found in the sugars and starches of foodstuffs. Fruits, potatoes, breads, sweets of all kinds, and milk products are abundant sources of fuel for muscle energy in the anaerobic stage of physical exertion[2] (that is, as the work being done begins to exceed the athlete's ability to provide enough oxygen to oxidize fuel rapidly enough to meet the need for energy at the required rate).

Fats are also present in foods in relatively large amounts and the fatty-acid needs of the body are met as long as sufficient food is taken in for energy-yielding purposes. Fats, which are known as lipids, are found in fatty meats, vegetable oils, and milk products. These compounds are stored in muscle tissue and in other deposits around the body, and are the primary source of fuel during mild (aerobic) exercise. Almost all normal energy comes from fats.[3]

Proteins are made up of amino acids which are utilized by the body for growth and repair. Proteins are not important as a source of fuel for muscle energy.[4] The proportion of protein in most foods is rather small, but those which are rich in the complex amino acids are meats, fish, nuts, whole grain cereals, eggs, beans, and milk products.

Inorganic salts are substances which are essential for growth, repair, and the regulation of certain body processes. Except under unusual circumstances, these minerals are present in the normal, balanced diet in amounts which meet the minimum daily requirements of the body.

Water plays an important role in almost every form of physiological activity. It is an indispensable solvent and diluting agent, it is used for the transportation of body fuels and waste products, and it serves as a key factor in regulating body temperature by removing excess heat. About two-thirds of the total body weight is water and if the water content of the body is reduced as much as ten percent, serious disorders will result. Thus, it is imperative that a balance be maintained between water intake and water loss, and this level is preserved primarily by feelings of thirst and satiety within the individual.

Vitamins are necessary for the maintenance of normal physiological functioning. These substances are complex organic compounds commonly present in foods, and a well-balanced diet will meet all of the vitamin needs of the body.

Diet.   Adequate nutrition for the girl athlete requires: (1) an amount of food which will maintain her weight at an optimum level; (2) a variety selected from foodstuffs which make up the balanced diet (dairy products, green and yellow vegetables, other vegetables, cereals and cereal

---

[2]From an interview with Dr. Theodore Van Itallie, "If Only We Knew," *Nutrition Today,* 3 (June, 1968), p. 5.

[3]*Ibid.*

[4]Per-Olof Åstrand, "Something Old and Something New . . . Very New," *Nutrition Today,* 3 (June, 1968), p. 9.

products, citrus and noncitrus fruits, and meats); and (3) regular eating habits. The athlete's diet should be composed of foods which she enjoys and which include carbohydrates, fats, proteins, mineral salts, water, and vitamins. Milk and eggs are especially desirable since they contain most of the substances necessary for the maintenance of physiological activities. The provision of an adequate supply of minerals and vitamins is of particular importance and both vegetables and fruits have special values in this regard, as well as in the supplying of indigestible cellulose which provides roughage to aid elimination.

If research tells us anything about diet for the athlete, it is that there are no nutritional shortcuts to performance excellence or to increased ability to do work. Throughout the training and playing seasons, the dream of a magic food must be put aside in favor of the well-balanced diet which includes all of the basic nutrients in proportions which correspond to the athlete's habitual eating pat ern. For optimum nutrition her diet must be both adequate and enjoyable.

Some coaches are opposed to fats in the diet of the girl athlete, but since fat is the substance which produces muscle energy during normal activity (under conditions of aerobic metabolism), such a restriction is contraindicated. Van Itallie suggests that as much as half of the calories in the high-calorie diet required by the athlete in training might be composed of fats, and he sees ". . . no reason to forego fat before a sports contest."[5]

Another unsupported conviction of many coaches is the belief that a high-protein diet will increase energy potential and that steak, or eggs, or whole grain cereal (or *something* basically protein in nature), is an essential pre-game food. While a high-protein diet will provide a necessary contribution to muscle growth during the early weeks of the training season, protein is not an energy producing food.

As exercise is prolonged, carbohydrates increase in importance as the oxygen supply becomes more inadequate, until finally, in anaerobic metabolism, all muscle energy is supplied from this source. Thus, the addition of increased proportions of carbohydrates to the usual amounts of fats and proteins in the diet is recommended for several days prior to each game. A carbohydrate-rich diet effects glycogen stores and will improve the capacity for prolonged exercise.[6]

The immediate pre-game meal should consist of anything the athlete wishes to eat, as long as the meal takes place three or four hours in advance of the game in order to permit the stomach to empty.

---

[5]Van Itallie, *op. cit.,* p. 6.
[6]Åstrand, *op. cit.,* p. 11.

Food Supplements. For many years medical nutritionists have known that the composition of the diet could enhance the capacity for prolonged exercise. To date, however, scientists have not supplied experimental evidence in support of the widely-held belief that food additives and dietary supplements can improve athletic performance. Although commercial producers of high protein-content additives and vitamin-rich supplements have avidly promoted this concept, exercise physiologists who have conducted research dealing with the nutrition of the athlete, maintain that such manipulations of an already well-balanced diet will have no positive effect on strength or endurance.

The claims for special protein supplements seem especially attractive to coaches and athletes, but as long ago as 1866 it was demonstrated that the combustion of protein was no higher during heavy exercise than during rest. This 100-year-old investigation has been verified repeatedly, and Åstrand tells us, ". . . as far as we know, a well-balanced diet of normal foods will provide all the protein an athlete needs for peak performance."[7] The claims of the producers of protein additives concerning their values are pseudoscientific at best, but clever advertising, accentuating the fact that muscle tissue is protein, results in the sale of additive tablets by the countless thousands.

The other currently popular myth is concerned with vitamins — in particular vitamins C and E. It is reported that some athletes use as much as 2500 mg of vitamin C per day (the minimum daily requirement is 50 mg)! Others ingest amazing quantities of vitamin E, despite the fact that the Senior Physician for the United States Olympic Teams has stated, "vitamin E has been used for everything from gray hair to infertility and heart disease and it hasn't altered the course of any of them very much."[8] And as Van Itallie and his co-researchers have pointed out:

> In spite of occasional reports of apparently beneficial effects of vitamin supplementation upon athletic performance, it remains to be demonstrated convincingly that supplementation of the diet of the athlete in training with vitamins of any sort has a beneficial effect on endurance, muscular efficiency, or coordination.[9]

---

[7] Ibid, p. 9.
[8] Daniel F. Hanley, "The Catastrophic Triviality," *Nutrition Today,* 3 (June, 1968), p. 20.
[9] Theodore B. Van Itallie, Leonardo Sinisterra, and Frederick J. Stare, "Nutrition and Athletic Performance, *Journal of the American Medical Association,* 162, (November 17, 1956), p. 1124.

In brief, nutritionists and knowledgeable athletic trainers assure us that a varied diet including green, yellow, and other vegetables; citrus and other fruits; milk products; meat and eggs; and breads and cereals will provide all the vitamins needed by the body. ". . . it is practically impossible for a normal healthy person living under ordinary circumstances to avoid the inclusion of adequate vitamins in his daily food intake."[10]

Salt Intake. Some of the essential minerals are present in the normal diet in larger amounts than are required by the body. Others, specifically, sodium, chlorine, calcium, phosphorus, iron, copper, and iodine, may not always be available in the usual foods in quantities sufficient to maintain certain body functions at an optimum level under abnormal conditions. The need for sodium and chlorine, for example, is ordinarily met by the sodium chloride (common table salt) naturally present in food and that which is added for seasoning. The normal intake of this mineral with food is from 10 to 15 grams per day. Under conditions which produce profuse or extended sweating, however, as much as 30 grams of sodium chloride may be excreted during the same period. While such conditions are conceivable, they also are extremely rare and the salt lost by basketball players through perspiration and urination ordinarily is replaced by the normal diet. In unusual instances where salt supplementation may be indicated, this need is met most effectively through increased food salting. The conventional practice of prescribing enteric salt tablets for basketball players throughout the training and competitive seasons is unnecessary and is more often the cause of nausea and impaired digestion than of meeting a valid mineral deficiency. ". . . there is no evidence to support the common practice of increasing the salt intake of athletes in excess of the losses that accompany sweating in normal competitive situations."[11]

Weight Control

Weight control is a matter of almost constant concern to all athletes, particularly during the off-season period. The necessary high-calorie diet of the training and competitive seasons tends to become habitual and many players continue to eat the same amount of food after the

---

[10]O. William Dayton, *Athletic Training and Conditioning* (New York: Ronald Press, Co., 1960), p. 33.
[11]Carl E. Klafs and Daniel D. Arnheim, *Modern Principles of Athletic Training* (St. Louis: C. V. Mosby Co., 1963), p. 115.

conclusion of the basketball season. The result is inevitably a weight gain due to the decrease in energy output (activity) which during the season had balanced the energy intake (food).

Overweight results from an excess of calories consumed over the calories expended. In the simplest terms, people who are overweight simply eat too much and exercise too little, and it is important that girl athletes understand the need for a sharp reduction in food intake immediately following the final basketball game of the season if they wish to avoid putting on pounds which will handicap them severely at the beach or pool during the ensuing summer.

Less frequently, the problem of weight control is one of being underweight. In this situation, too, the solution lies in the application of the balanced energy principle. The girl who wants to gain weight can only do so by raising the energy intake above the energy output. This can be done by increasing the amount of the *same kinds* of foods in the normal diet, or by augmenting the amounts of fats and other high-calorie foodstuffs in the *same amount* of food regularly eaten.

A girl's weight is the best indicator of energy balance. A constant body weight indicates that the energy supplied through the girl's diet is balanced by that lost through the sum total of her activities no matter what the degree of strenuousness of her exercise program. Weight loss is the result of a greater expenditure of energy than that supplied by the food intake. A gain in weight, on the other hand, indicates an unbalance in favor of the energy value of the ingested food. Ideally, the weight of the girl athlete during the off-season should not vary too much from her best playing weight unless she is still growing. In this case, fat deposits and muscle tone can be used as energy balance indicators.

When weight is used to check energy balance it should be recorded at approximately the same time each day, and prior to any prolonged, vigorous exercise.

MENSTRUATION

Despite literature which still indicates a rather wide variance of opinion regarding the desirability of strenuous exercise during menstruation, the issue is no longer a significant one in women's athletic programs. The development and maintenance of the high level of skill and physical condition required to compete successfully with other women athletes in the sports world of today demands regular, unbroken practice patterns, and dictates that those who aspire to such ends must continue their training and competitive programs through all phases of the menstrual cycle. In general, *all* women, the world over, who participate seriously in sports follow such a regimen.

Although present-day medical science informs us that regular, vigorous exercise has a beneficial effect on menstruation, in the past many physicians recommended that exercise should be curtailed during this period. Unfortunately, widespread misunderstanding of the menstrual function still exists and many coaches and athletes lack assurance as to the proper course of action concerning participation in conditioning activities and competition during menstruation.

In general, current medical opinion is reflected in a report published by the Research Committee of the DGWS in 1959,[12] which concluded that if the athlete is able to participate in training and competition during her menstrual period without dysmenorrhea or other menstrual-related disturbances, there is no reason to discontinue or restrict such activity during any phase of the menstrual cycle. This conclusion is supported by Erdelyi's summary of studies dealing with the problem, but he adds a further precautionary restriction: "The female athlete may continue her usual sports activities during her menstrual period . . . if her sports performance during the period is not worse than her usual average."[13] Erdelyi suggests that such a drop in performance may indicate that the girl cannot stand the increased stress that the sport requires from her during menstruation, and in such cases of apparent overstrain, he recommends the avoidance of competition or heavy training.

In regard to performance, a study of 729 Hungarian female athletes indicated that about half of the subjects showed no change in athletic performance during the menstrual period, about one-third declined in performance, while the performance of the remainder improved.[14] "Generally," writes Erdelyi, "the performances during the period are influenced more by psychological than by physical factors."[15]

Jokl, in his study of the performance of female athletes at the 1956 Melbourne Olympic Games, reported that at least six gold medals were won in swimming and track and field by women during the menstrual period.[16] These particular women obviously experienced little

---

[12]Marjorie Phillips, Katherine Fox, and Olive Young. "Sports Activities for Girls," *JOHPER,* 30 (December, 1959), pp. 23-25, 54.

[13]Gyula J. Erdelyi, "Women in Athletics," *Proceedings of the Second Conference on the Medical Aspects of Sports* (Washington: American Medical Association. 1960), p. 62.

[14]*Ibid.,* p. 61.

[15]*Ibid.*

[16]Ernst Jokl, "La Situation Athletique des Femmes," *Sport,* 22 (April, 1963), p. 110.

disadvantaged due to this factor. Jokl's report also indicated that apparently no contestants failed to compete in any event because of menstruation.

CHAPTER III

SHOOTING AND PASSING FUNDAMENTALS

SHOOTING

Since scoring in basketball depends upon the ability to put the ball in the basket, shooting is *the* indispensable skill of the game. All other offensive techniques are developed solely for the purpose of placing a player in a favorable position from which to attempt a shot at the basket. It follows that other aspects of the game contribute little toward the ultimate object of winning unless the players have developed effective shooting techniques. The best shooting team will usually win over teams possessing greater skill in other fundamentals. For this reason, beginners, novice players, and experts all invariably — and quite properly — devote more practice time to shooting than to the development and improvement of other individual fundamentals.

Shooting techniques have been perfected in an endless variation of styles over the years, but gradually, since its introduction and popularization (in the late 1930s) by the all-time great, Angelo "Hank" Luisetti of Stanford University, the one-handed shot has become the basic one in basketball. Short shots, long shots, lay-ups, pivot shots, free throws, and running shots from all angles and court positions can be taken with the same fundamental technique, and key moves of this procedure provide the logical starting point for teaching shooting skills.

The Basic One-Handed Set Shot

Set shots may be defined as those in which a player makes an attempt to score from a non-moving position on the court. Such shots using the basic one-handed technique may be taken from any spot on the court but under normal circumstances are most commonly made from within a radius of 20 feet from the basket.

In making the one-handed set shot with the right hand the ball is brought with both hands to a chin-high position eight to twelve inches in front of the face and slightly to the right of the vertical mid-line of the body (left-handed players will hold the ball slightly to the left of the body median). The shooting hand is behind and slightly under the ball, with the fingers pointed up and the wrist cocked back. The thumb is almost at right angles to the other fingers and is positioned so as to provide maximum hand control of the ball during the arm extension which provides the shooting force. The opposite hand is under the front of the ball in a cupping position, fingers pointed forward, primarily for support until the shot is initiated. The foot on the shooting hand side of the body is forward of the other foot and points in the direction of the basket (see Fig. 3-1).

For all intents and purposes, the several movements involved in assuming the above body position are made simultaneously and at the same time the knees are flexed, lowering the body into the firing position. The actual shooting motion is a push — similar to a shot-putting action — initiated by an extension of the shooting arm and the uncocking of the wrist through its full range of motion. The fingers maintain contact with the ball, providing directional control throughout the arm extension. Following the release, the arm follows-through in the direction of the ball flight (see Fig. 3-2).

Wrist and finger control is the double key to accuracy in making the one-handed shot. While the main source of the force needed to shoot the ball comes from the large muscles of the legs and the arms, and the general direction in which this force is applied comes from body position and the direction of the push given by the arm extension, final adjustments in both the propelling force and the ball flight direction are made with the wrist and fingers. Baskets are made with the small muscles of arm and hand, and one's degree of skill in shooting is a measure of her learned ability to control wrist and finger action with fine precision.

As the distance of the attempted shot increases, more power must be applied through the legs and trunk, and players usually leave the floor from the force of the extension of the legs when shooting from twenty or more feet from the basket. Some players habitually leave the floor in this manner even on short shots.

Free Throws.   No shot in the game is as easy from a mechanical point of view as the free throw — a 15-foot, unhurried, straight shot with no defensive player attempting to block or impede the effort — and yet the team which loses in close games invariably does so on the basis of missed foul shots! It is imperative that a great deal of time be devoted to the practicing of free throws and preferably such practice should be so frequent and so regular that the successful execution of the shot becomes almost automatic. Free throws are "gifts" in this game, and the coach should attempt to develop a team attitude which will not concede the possibility of missed foul shots.

The one-handed set shot technique should always be used in taking free throws and each player should routinize each aspect of the shot. The girl taking free throws in either practice sessions or in a game

FIGURE 3-1   Shooting position for the basic one-handed shot.

situation, should be precisely habitual in the placement of her feet, in the position of the hands in holding the ball, in the time span used in completing the shot, and in the body movements involved in executing the action from start to follow-through.

The Jump Shot. The jump shot (the jumper) is a version of the one-handed set shot which has gained wide popularity because of the difficulty in effectively guarding against it. The execution of this shot is similar to the standard set shot technique, except that the ball is brought

FIGURE 3-2 *Body position at release of the basic one-handed set shot. Note wrist snap and follow-through.*

to a shooting position above the head instead of in front of the face, and it is released at the highest point of a vertical jump from the floor (see Fig. 3-3).

The One-Handed Running Shot

Except that it is made while the player is in motion, usually as the culmination of a dribble, the one-handed running shot is basically the same as the standard set shot. The ball is lifted with both hands to the shooting position in front of the face while the weight of the body is

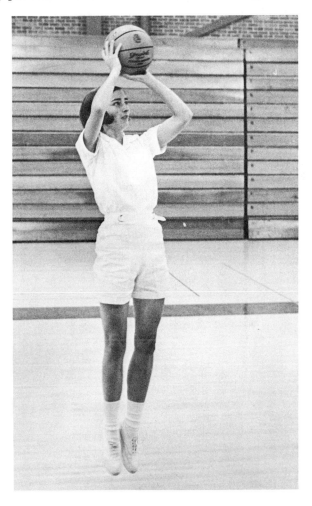

FIGURE 3-3   Shooting position for the one-handed jump shot.

passing over the outside foot (the foot away from the basket). Since the take-off for a running one-handed shot should always be made from the inside foot, the knee of that leg is flexed in preparation for the subsequent take-off jump as the inside foot touches down.

Unless the direction of travel of the player is directly toward the basket, the take-off should be an upward and forward drive combined with a turn which faces the girl toward such a heading. This jump and turn toward the basket, and the normal subsequent forward swing of the opposite leg, places the shooter in the basic firing position for the shot — and with a height advantage several feet better than par.

FIGURE 3-4   Release of the one-handed running shot. Note height advantage.

The ball is held with the shooting hand (the hand away from the basket) under and behind the ball. The supporting hand in the running shot is in front of the ball rather than cupped underneath the ball as in the set shot.

The shot is made at the top of the jump from the take-off leg by a forward extension of the arm pushing the ball into the desired trajectory. Wrist snap provides the final impetus for the ball, and control is maintained by finger contact until release (see Fig. 3-4).

The Lay-Up Shot. The lay-up (often called a set-up or crip shot) is a one-handed running shot taken from under the basket, usually at the conclusion of a drive-in. In order to improve the odds on making this shot, the player attempts to reduce the flight path of the ball to an absolute minimum by getting as high into the air as possible on the final stride from the take-off leg, and by releasing the ball from over the head at the peak of this take-off stride. The ball is carried almost to the release point with both hands, and at the peak of the jump stride the outside arm is further extended in an effort to lay the ball against the backboard in such a manner that it will carom into the basket (see Fig. 3-5).

Nowhere in the game is the advantage of being able to shoot with both hands more evident than in the execution of the lay-up. Assuming that the members of the opposing team are doing an effective defensive job, they will always attempt to have a guarding player between the girl with the ball and the basket. This means that the offensive player usually will not be able to shoot with her inside hand without offering an easily blocked shot, and since shooting the ball with the outside hand implies the use of the left as often as the right, all players should work on this shot with both hands until they can score with it from either side of the court with a high degree of consistency.

The Two-Handed Set Shot

The two-handed shot has two advantages over the basic one-handed technique which make it a worthwhile skill for the player to acquire. First, it provides more power and consequently is a highly useful form to use with shots taken from 25 to 40 feet from the basket. In certain situations, such as in the closing seconds of a game or a playing period, it is frequently quite desirable for a player to be able to take a long shot with some chance of scoring. Second, since the two-handed shot begins from the standard position of readiness, it is usually possible to get it off quicker than the one-handed set shot — especially with short-or medium-range attempts which require only wrist and forearm action.

In the position of readiness prior to executing the shot, the hands are placed slightly behind and slightly on top of the ball with the fingers comfortably spread and the thumbs pointed toward each other. The ball is held chest high primarily by finger tip pressure. Foot placement varies with individuals and is usually dictated by the stance the player habitually assumes in the position of readiness (in the days when this shot was the "standard" form, eastern players often took it with the feet together, while westerners were more prone to a stance in which one foot was in advance of the other). In any case, balance is the essential objective in foot placement.

FIGURE 3-5   Shooting position for the lay-up shot. Note shooting hand position and upward lift of body.

In taking the shot, the body is lowered by bending the knees, the wrists are dropped, and the ball is lofted by a forceful straightening of the legs and arms. The hands follow-through after the ball, and the wrists rotate inward as the ball is released (see Fig. 3-6).

Many players habitually drop into a flexed knees position whenever they make a stop, which obviously increases the effectiveness of their position of readiness since it provides better ball protection and enables them to take a two-handed shot without the delay involved in the necessary prerequisite of having to lower the body from a more erect position.

FIGURE 3-6   Release of the two-handed set shot. Note follow-through and inward wrist rotation.

The Hook Shot

When properly employed, the hook shot is almost impossible to guard against effectively without fouling and, consequently, it is a most desirable skill for any player to develop. It is an especially useful shot for forwards to master, since it is used primarily in a situation in which the girl with the ball is close to the goal, has her back to the basket, and is being guarded aggressively from the rear by a defensive player — a typical game situation deep in the front court.

In executing the basic hook shot from such a stopped position the

FIGURE 3-7   Release of the hook shot. Note ball position behind head.

player takes a step toward the back court (usually on an appropriate radial from the basket), leading with the leg on the side toward which she plans to make the subsequent turn back toward the goal. As this stride is taken, the head is turned in the direction of the stride so that the player is looking back over her shoulder at the target basket.

This initial step has a two-fold purpose: it moves the shootér away from her guard and the normally congested area under or near the basket, and it provides helpful momentum for the necessary subsequent action.

As the step is completed the weight is shifted over the touchdown foot, and the body is pivoted to a position in which the inside shoulder points toward the basket. The eyes have remained focused on the basket, and at this phase of the sequence the shooter is looking at the target laterally across her inside shoulder.

During the pivot the ball is cupped in the hand of the outside arm and carried laterally upward in a slinging movement (the shot gets its name for this "hooking" motion) by a sweeping abduction of the arm. This arm swing is timed so that the release of the ball is made above and behind the head and at the high point of the spring from the pivot foot. Finger control is maintained, as with all shots, until the instant of release (see Fig. 3-7).

The hook shot is not limited to the stride-away-from-the-basket-and-pivot technique described above, although this usage is the basic form and the only recommended employment of the shot except by extremely experienced players. A slinging shot taken laterally over the head can, of course, be made from practically any conceivable floor and/or body position, but with the typical player the accuracy of this involved coordination is usually so poor that such a shot invariably becomes a questionable tactic. Under normal circumstances, if a player is in a position other than the one described, and a standard one-handed shot cannot be made, the ball should be passed out rather than hooked.

The Two-Handed Overhead Shot

Many tall players have become adept at increasing their natural advantage by the frequent use of the two-handed overhead shot. This shot is very difficult to block and it can be taken very quickly from the initial overhead position. Some coaches, as matter of fact, have been so impressed by the benefits of this initial position that they have given serious consideration to the idea of teaching it as the primary position of readiness when the player has already used her dribble option. Its chief weakness in this regard — and it is a most serious one when used by short players, or even those of average height — is in the absence of the body protection afforded the ball in the more commonly used standard position of readiness.

The first move is to bring the ball to the initial position above and in front of the head with both hands. The hands are behind and slightly under the ball with the fingers spread comfortably and the thumbs pointed toward each other. The arms are flexed so that the elbows, which are spread wider than the shoulders, are forward of the hands (see Fig. 3-8). From this position, the shot is initiated by increas-

FIGURE 3-8   Shooting position for the two-handed overhead shot.

ing the flexion of the elbows and cocking the wrists back. Impetus is provided by a forward extension of the forearms and wrists. The fingers provide final control and the arms follow-through in the direction of the shot.

A popular variation of the overhead shot which is used most effectively by some athletes, is the addition of a vertical jump prior to the release of the ball (see Fig. 3-9). The height advantage thus gained is obviously a significant one and this technique is a valuable accessory to any basketball player's repertoire of shooting skills.

FIGURE 3-9   Shooting position for the two-handed overhead jump shot.

Coaching Hints for Improving Shooting Performance

1. Under usual circumstances, with all shots except lay-ups, the player should shoot for the basket rather than attempting to carom the ball off the backboard. Banking shots is doing it the hard way, simply because each backboard reacts differently.
2. Experienced players focus their eyes on the near rim of the basket while shooting, and concentrate on an attempt to drop the ball just over the edge of this target.
3. Being able to shoot one-handed set and running shots with either hand gives one a tremendous advantage in this game, and all players should devote a great deal of practice to the acquiring and maintaining of such ambidextrous skills.
4. In practice, beginners and novice players should accentuate the follow-through on all shots. Make sure that the wrists rotate the hands inward as the ball is released. While the follow-through adds nothing mechanically to the flight of the ball, this habitual action will greatly increase the effectiveness of the complex coordinations which take place during the prerelease phase of any shot.
5. While practicing shooting, a common mistake of inexperienced players is to shoot from too far out. During a game, shots are seldom attempted from further than 20 feet, and simply for this rather estimable reason, shooting during practice sessions should be limited largely to within this radius of the goal. For some strange reason this is a difficult concept to get across to players. Some coaches find it advantageous to chalk, tape, or whitewash a 20-foot range limit arc on the floor at each basket during the first several weeks of practice in order to promote the habit of practicing shooting skills at game situation distances.
6. Girls should learn the various techniques by first working at short range and gradually increasing the distance. In all shooting practice the player should be able to concentrate on form without having to be concerned with reaching the goal. Basket shooting is not a strength event, and the ability to project the ball to the basket from a normal shooting distance is largely a matter of technique. When a girl is conscious of pressing to reach the basket, she is taking a shot which is too long. The best shooting form is an effortless one.
7. One plays the game in the manner she practices. Players should practice with concentration, making a real effort to sink every attempted shot. A worthwhile attitude to develop is one which makes every practice floor shot a crucial one; every practice free throw a game winner; every practice lay-up a last second tie breaker.

PASSING

In any conceivable hierarchy of basic skills, shooting obviously must be considered the essential fundamental of basketball. However, since even the highest degree of this ability is useless unless the ball can first be brought into a scoring position, the importance of the skills required to pass the ball effectively — that is, quickly and accurately against various defensive situations — cannot be overemphasized. Basketball is a game in which each player must be able to move the ball with a variety of techniques, and the adequate development of these estimable skills calls for endless practice.

Many individual styles of passing have been perfected, but five types are basic to all variations: The two-handed chest pass, the one-handed pass, the bounce pass, the hook pass, and the two-handed overhead pass. The acquisition of the skills required to make these passes will provide the player with the ability to move the ball efficiently and effectively in any conceivable game situation.

The Two-Handed Chest Pass

The key pass in basketball is the chest pass simply because the experienced player in possession of the ball, and not in motion, habitually assumes the position of readiness (see Fig. 3-10). From this

FIGURE 3-10   Position of readiness. Note body balance. Player is in position to pass, dribble, or shoot.

stance the player is in the initial position for the execution of the two-handed pass. The ball is held with both hands in front of the body on a level between the waist and the shoulders. The hands are on the side of, and slightly behind, the ball, with the fingers spread comfortably and the thumbs pointed toward each other. The ball is held by the fingertips, with the hands being slightly cupped so that the palms do not touch the cover of the ball.

The pass is executed by drawing the ball in toward the body, dropping the wrists, and pushing the ball directly outward with both arms. As the arms are extended in a follow-through in the direction of the pass, the wrists rotate bringing the thumbs of the hands inward (see Fig. 3-11). As in shooting, the fingers provide final directional control and force adjustments. Normally, with the extension of the arms there is a shift of body weight from the rear to the forward leg. However, since the chest pass is used primarily for relatively short throws, it

FIGURE 3-11   body position at release of the chest pass. Note follow-through and inward wrist rotation.

becomes basically an arm, wrist, and finger action with experienced players, and often is made without any noticeable shift of weight from the balanced position of readiness.

The One-Handed Pass

This pass is used extensively by experienced players for both short and long passes, and is the recommended technique for all long throws.

The initial move in making this pass is to shift the ball to a head-high position on the throwing arm side of the body. The throwing hand is behind the ball with the fingers up, the wrist is cocked back, and the elbow is behind the ball. Normally, the foot on the opposite side of the body is forward of the other foot and pointed in the direction of the anticipated pass. From this position the toss is made by a normal overhand throwing motion. Hips and shoulders lead the throw and the arm follows-through in the direction of the throw.

When executed as a short pass, the throwing hand is not drawn back to the shoulder. The ball is held forward of the ear just prior to the throw, and the action is primarily a forearm, wrist, and finger motion. For longer throws, more arm and body strength are required to produce the needed power and the long one-handed pass is usually called a "baseball pass" from the fact that it is made with a baseball-like throwing motion from a beginning position well behind the head (see Fig. 3-12).

Frequently, the one-handed pass is thrown in a lateral direction across the front of the body. In executing this movement the upper body is rotated in the direction of the pass as the arm is cocked and the ball is brought up to the initial position beside the face. This action places the shoulder girdle in a position similar to that used in the straightaway pass previously described.

Some players become very skillful with the use of a deceptive tactic in connection with this lateral pass by not looking in the direction of the intended throw. This deception is furthered by limiting the upper body rotation and making the pass a true cross-body motion thrown largely with the arm and hand.

For maximum effectiveness, it is essential that the player be able to execute the short one-handed pass with either hand and the novice should constantly practice this fundamental movement from both sides of the body.

The Bounce Pass

The name commonly given to this pass is a misleading one. A slide pass would be a more descriptive label for this action. The ball does carom off the playing floor during its travel between two players, but without a skidding action such floor contact will only slow the flight of the ball making it more vulnerable to possible interception by the defense. The secret of the good bounce pass is in the development of the ability to slide or skid the ball off the floor much in the manner of a flat stone being skipped on the surface of a pond. The pass *must not* bounce — it must skid flatly across the floor without appreciable loss of momentum.

Bounce passes are used primarily to get the ball past a defensive player stationed between the passer and the receiver and except under

FIGURE 3-12   Throwing position for the one-handed pass.

unusual circumstances, are employed only for relatively short distances. This technique can be used effectively with the two-handed chest pass or with a one-handed pass from either side of the body.

Normally, the two-handed bounce pass is executed from the position of readiness, and it is made in a manner similar to the standard chest pass in all respects except that the bounce pass action commences from a lower body position in order to facilitate the skidding floor contact in the flight path of the ball. This lowering of the release point is accomplished by taking a stride in the direction of the throw and simultaneously flexing the knees. As the stride is started the ball is pulled back toward the body, the wrists are dropped, and the ball pushed forward by a vigorous extension of the arms. As always, the ball is held initially with the fingers. As the arms are extended in the follow-through, the wrists rotate inward turning the thumbs downward.

The one-handed bounce pass is made with a low side arm motion in order to keep the trajectory of the ball as flat as possible. As with the two-handed variation, the pass is normally initiated from the position of readiness and the action invariably begins with a stride. In this case, however, the step is a lateral one rather than in the direction of the planned throw (this initial movement can be either a cross-body or a side step), and it is made for the purpose of gaining a more favorable angle from which to slide the ball past a close defensive player. As the lateral stride is taken, the ball is brought back past the hip on that side of the body. The throw is initiated with a sweeping forward motion of the arm on a low horizontal plane (see Fig. 3-13). The hand is behind the ball throughout the motion, and at the release of the ball, the wrist and fingers provide final impetus and control. To use the one-handed bounce pass with maximum effectiveness, the player must learn to make the throw with either hand.

The Hook Pass

The primary use of the hook pass is to clear the ball from a congested area in which the use of other techniques might involve a greater risk of losing the ball to the opponents. It is particularly useful in clearing the ball from under the defensive basket.

The execution of the hook pass is similar to the technique previously described for the hook shot. The player initiates the action by taking a stride away from the area of congestion, pivoting 90° on the lead foot to place the body (specifically the shoulder girdle) in a lateral position with reference to the direction of the intended pass, and hooking the ball with the characteristic upward lateral swinging motion of the arm (see Fig. 3-14). The trajectory of the hook pass is controlled by the hand, and is kept relatively flat. The actual flight path of the ball is generally downward, starting as high as possible from above and behind the passer's head, and reaching the receiver between chest and head height.

The Two-Handed Overhead Pass

The technique employed in executing this pass is identical with that used in the two-handed overhead shot, and it has similar advantages —

FIGURE 3-13   Execution of the one-handed bounce pass. Note knee flexion and body lean to lower release point.

it is very difficult to block because of the height from which it is thrown, and it can be executed very quickly because of the few preliminary movements necessary prior to release. The initial position for this pass provides an additional benefit in that the passer is able to fake the intended direction of the throw effectively with very limited motion of the arms alone.

The pass is thrown from an initial position in which the ball is held above and in front of the head with the finger tips of both hands. The arms are in a flexed position, placing the elbows forward of the hands. The thumbs are pointed toward each other. In executing the shot the elbow flexion is increased and the wrists are cocked, followed

FIGURE 3-14   Release of the hook pass.

immediately by a forward extension of the forearms and wrists. As in all passes, the fingers provide final control and the arms follow-through in the direction of the throw (see Fig. 3-15).

The weaknesses of this pass are both inherent in the starting point of the throw. It is a relatively poor position of readiness from which to execute a dribble or any other offensive maneuver except the overhead pass or shot, and except when used by players who are considerably taller than their opponents, the ball is exposed in a very vulnerable manner. Because of this latter reason, experienced athletes seldom

FIGURE 3-15   Release of the two-handed overhead pass.

employ this position of readiness unless they are sure that there are no defensive players behind them.

Coaching Hints for Improving Passing Performance

1. Beginners should practice the fundamental passes by working with a partner at a distance of 12-15 feet.

2. The preferred target of any pass should be at a point where the receiver can handle it best. This will vary, of course, depending upon the floor situation. At first, however, while learning the skills the passer should use her partner's chest as a target. Some coaches teach beginners to throw all passes so that the ball arrives at the receiver at the same height from which the pass was originated.

3. The trajectory of all passes should be kept as flat as possible in order to decrease the time that the ball is in the air between passer and receiver. Obviously, every additional fraction of a second that the ball is not under positive control of the offensive team increases the opportunity of the defense to make an interception.

4. The nature of the game is such that accurate passes and catches must be made while the players are in motion. As skill is developed, therefore, players must learn to pass and catch the ball while on the run. The judgment factor involved in throwing to a moving target with proper lead is one of the key factors which determines the success of individual performance in passing.

CHAPTER IV

DRIBBLING AND FOOTWORK FUNDAMENTALS

DRIBBLING

For the first five or six decades of the game, the use of the dribble was a controversial issue in basketball. Rules regarding this means of moving the ball varied widely over these years, but as the modern game evolved the trend was steadily toward its unlimited use as a potent offensive maneuver. The appeal of dribbling lies in the fact that it is an aspect of basketball which involves a real one-against-one challenge. Dribbling is inherently a highly charged, competitive action in a game which was designed deliberately to avoid rough and combative play. Essentially, it is a basic challenge between two individuals in which one player says, in effect, "I'm going to move this ball past you," and the opponent says, "try and do it!" Such a confrontation touches a primeval element of human nature and dribbling is exciting to both player and spectator. There is little doubt that the dribble option adds a dramatic element to basketball which has contributed immeasurably to its worldwide appeal.

Of course, when the dribble is improperly used — as it so often is with inexperienced players — the maneuver can be quite detrimental to the game. A contest which involves excessive, inexpedient bouncing of the ball is an effective way to convert one of the most exciting sports into a dull, uninteresting activity for both player and spectator.

Properly used, the dribble has five purposes, each of which has the potential of contributing spectacularly to the offensive phase of the game:

1. The dribble is an essential maneuver in driving in for a lay-up shot. In every game numerous situations arise in which an offensive player

with the ball has a short-lived, unobstructed path to the goal, and at an early stage in their basketball experience, girls must acquire the dribbling skill necessary to capitalize on these opportunities.

2. The dribble is used to move the ball in situations where a pass is inappropriate. For example, frequently all potential pass receivers are covered so well that a pass would entail an untenable risk of interception. At other times, the available receivers are in such poor floor positions that a pass to any one of them would slow down or detract from the offensive potential of the moment.

3. The dribble is often used to clear the ball from a congested area from which a pass cannot be safely initiated. Such a situation is not uncommon after a successful rebound by a defensive player under her backboard. Similarly, it is sometimes essential for a hemmed-in offensive player to be able to clear herself by dribbling out from under the front court basket.

4. The dribble is occasionally used as a means of spreading the defense. Although such a maneuver normally is quite futile against a zone, a skilled offensive dribbler can be extremely effective in setting-up man-to-man alignments by forcing a sagging defensive player to commit herself primarily to the ball, thus, giving an advantage to the girl she was guarding.

5. The dribble is regularly used to go around a weaker defensive opponent. If an offensive player discovers that she has the ability to fake her guard into an off-balance position and dribble by her, such a tactic should be exploited whenever the opportunity to thus move the ball into a more favorable court position presents itself.

Although the technique involved in dribbling a basketball appears to be rather simple and straightforward, it is in reality a very complex maneuver. There are relatively few top-flight dribblers (among either men or women) simply because few basketball players devote practice time to the development of this skill with the same dedication given to other fundamentals of the game such as shooting and passing. It is the most overlooked and underrated basic skill of the game — by coaches and players alike.

The dribble is a technique in which the ball is bounced by light touches of the fleshy pads of the first joints of the fingers. Properly executed, the impetus is a stroking motion, not a slapping or striking at the ball, and except as a possible incidental follow-through, the base of the fingers and the palm of the hand should not contact the ball in the action. The dribbling technique requires that the fingers and wrist of the dribbling hand be loose and relaxed in order to achieve the suppleness required for the execution of the proper caressing-like motion (see Fig. 4-1).

The ball should never be dribbled unless the player is moving. Standing in place and bouncing the ball is a useless maneuver which simply invites a more experienced opponent to attempt to steal the ball. When dribbling, the ball must be kept far enough in front of the body to avoid kicking it inadvertently, but protection of the ball is the primary factor which must influence this distance. Similarly, the height of the bounce varies from knee-high to waist-high depending upon the floor situation and the related need for ball protection. When moving the ball rapidly, the dribble is relatively high and the body is kept in a more upright position than when protecting the ball is the primary objective. In the latter case the dribble is kept low and

FIGURE 4-1   Initiating the dribble. Note head position and hand action.

the bounce is closer to the body in order to facilitate the shielding of the ball.

Novice players invariably find it necessary to watch the ball while dribbling, which naturally results in loss of visual contact with the immediate playing situation. As soon as possible in her sports career, the young basketball player must acquire the ability to control the dribble and still keep her head up. Among basketball players the commonly used admonition, "heads up!" is more than an order for mental alertness. It literally refers to a basic requisite of the game — the necessity of maintaining visual concentration on the developing game situation at all times.

Since a player in possession of the ball should always use her body as a screen between the ball and the nearest defensive player, an essential refinement of the basic skill is the ability to dribble effectively with either hand and on either side of the body (see Fig. 4-2).

FIGURE 4-2 Protecting the ball while dribbling.

Coaching Hints for Improving Dribbling Skill

1. As an obvious first step in learning to dribble, the beginner must learn to bounce the ball. Initially, she will have to watch the ball, keep it well away from her body, and maintain a relatively erect position in order to control its action.
2. From the earliest stages in this learning process, attention must be concentrated on the development of the stroking motion of the dribbling hand. The novice should think of "petting" the ball rather than hitting it.
3. While developing the dribbling technique, beginners should practice bouncing the ball in place with both right and left hand. It is not without reason that the ability to use either hand in the execution of basic fundamental skills is a key mark of the good basketball player.
4. As bouncing skill increases, the coach should add the element of having the players dribble without looking at the ball. Begin with drills in which the ball is bounced in place while the girls move their heads from side to side, focusing their visual attention on other activities taking place around the gym. The attempt should be to keep the bounce of the ball within sight without looking directly at it. The range of one's peripheral vision can be markedly extended through practice and such increase in visual acuity is a most praiseworthy goal for any athlete.
5. As soon as the player begins to acquire some degree of skill in bouncing the ball with a relaxed hand and without staring at it, locomotion should be added to the drills. Start with a walking dribble and increase the speed of movement as rapidly as the girl can learn to control the ball.
6. Because ball position is a most important aspect of effective dribbling, the player must learn to dribble low for maximum ball protection and somewhat higher for maximum speed of movement. The ball must be protected as much as possible through using the body as a screen in crowded areas of the court, so it is necessary for players to learn to dribble the ball on either side of the body. Drills which call for constant shifts of the ball relative to body position — from right side to front to left side — are invaluable learning aids as the players become increasingly proficient at this spectacular aspect of the game.

FOOTWORK FUNDAMENTALS

Basketball is a game characterized by movement to a degree found in few other team sports. Player mobility is the essence of the game and team success is dependent in a very real sense upon the ability of the players to move effectively and rapidly. Thus, the skill of running is the basic footwork fundamental. Other skills included among the so-called footwork fundamentals are the ability to stop running without violating the rule against traveling with the ball, the ability to maneuver away from a defensive opponent through pivoting, and the several locomotor techniques involved in individual defensive tactics.

Running Forward

Although running is often spoken of as a "natural" movement, there are few people other than athletes or ex-athletes who actually are able to move effectively or efficiently at any pace above a moderate walk. This is because running is actually a very complex skill — one which does not come naturally to anyone. Good running form must be learned like any other motor skill and, unfortunately, few children receive any training in the proper technique of this activity at any phase of the physical education to which they are exposed. It is particularly deplorable that except in those few schools which have competitive track and field programs for coeds, virtually no girls receive specific instruction in running during early adolescence. The need for such basic physical education at this stage of development is grounded in the fact that as the young woman matures, the pelvis widens resulting in an obliquity of the thigh bones. This factor brings about a sideways shift of the center of gravity with each stride as the girl moves and most females run with a pronounced lateral sway of the pelvis.

Girls who are not taught proper leg and arm motion at this stage of their growth usually develop awkward running movement patterns in their attempts (often subconsciously) to offset the hip sway. The most commonly seen compensation is an outward throw of the lower leg and foot during the forward movement of each stride. This action rotates the femur inward adding a handicapping twisting motion of the trunk to the already grossly ineffectual outward cast of the lower limb. Another familiar attempt to compensate for lateral body sway is a running position in which the upper arms are held tightly against the sides and the lower arms are thrown outward from the elbows with each stride.

To reduce the natural running disadvantage inherent in feminine anatomy, basketball players should drill frequently on proper running form in which compensatory movement patterns are replaced by a high, straightforward knee lift and by an arm motion emphasizing a free swing from the shoulder joint.

The type of running required in playing basketball is clearly not the same thing as the classic style used by the track athlete. There are, however, certain mechanical aspects which are common to each of the many variations of running style employed in different sports, and these basic patterns must become habitual before any girl is really ready to begin learning the specific refinements of running called for in basketball.

Although back leg push provides the forward motion of the body in running, the action of the lead leg is the factor which needs attention with most untrained girl runners. The front leg must be lifted, moved forward, and placed down in a vertical plane and in a straight line. Any tendency toward an outward throw of the lower leg as the knee is lifted with each stride must be avoided, and the foot should not be allowed to toe in or toe out as it is placed down. The feet should strike the floor with enough lateral spread to maintain adequate body balance for possible sudden changes in direction.

Arm action in running is another common mechanical error with most girls. In normal running, the arms swing in opposition to the leg action and they should swing freely from the shoulders with whatever elbow flexion feels natural. The common error of holding the upper arms against the sides and throwing the lower arms outward from the elbows should be eliminated early in the girl's athletic career. The correct motion of the arm swing is obliquely across the body in a forward and backward direction.

Running Backwards

One other aspect of running must be stressed as a fundamental footwork skill for basketball players. The ability to run backwards is an invaluable defensive technique and only of slightly lesser importance in certain offensive situations. Defensively, it is advantageous for players of the team which has just lost the ball to back pedal to their defensive floor positions if they are not being outraced by a fast break. The obvious plus factor of running backwards is that the defensive players thus maintain visual orientation with the developing playing situation. Loss of this vital awareness, which invariably occurs when a player turns her back on the advancing ball to run to her defensive position, calls for a reorientation when she again faces the offensive team. These few seconds of being "tuned out" can give an alert offensive team a decided — even though momentary — advantage. And advantages are something no defensive unit can afford to give up easily. The offense already has more than its share of such!

On offense, the same general rationale applies. It's just smart basketball to keep aware of the game situation constantly. Basketball is a game in which breaks (good ones and bad ones) occur frequently and in extremely short time spans, and even the briefest lapses of visual contact can have a most detrimental influence on team effectiveness. Unless a fast break is being used to bring the ball down court, the offensive front players should maintain maximum visual contact with the rest of the floor — particularly with their teammates advancing the ball. Back court players are often challenged by a sudden press and it is not at all unusual for the ball-handler in such a situation to need help quickly. At other times while the ball is being advanced, unexpected, short-lived offensive opportunities occur. Many scoring possibilities are lost in almost all schoolgirl games due to a player proceeding down court with her back to the playing situation.

As a general rule of thumb, all players, both offensive and defensive, should strive to keep the ball in view at all times. There simply is no other way to know what's going on at any particular moment and such knowledge is invaluable in this game. The ability to run backwards is an essential skill in meeting this need.

Running backwards is an unnatural form of locomotion which requires movement patterns quite unlike those used in normal running. As in forward progress, the problem is one of maintaining balance. Because of body structure, however, the technique involved is contrary to natural instincts and thus is an entirely different skill.

In forward running, as speed is increased the center of gravity moves ahead of the feet due to the increase in body lean, placing the person in a state of unstable equilibrium. The knee joint normally prevents this situation from developing into an off-balance catastrophe by providing the runner with the potential of getting a supporting leg back under the hips with each stride in time to maintain a stable attitude. When a runner falls, it is because she has been unable to prevent the unstable condition from proceeding beyond the recovery point. Successful running is actually a series of narrowly averted sprawls as the center of gravity shifts with every stride to a point just short of the limit at which balance can be maintained.

Most girls have never learned to run backwards and when they attempt to do so their center of gravity tends to move in the backward direction faster than their feet. Being unable to counteract this tendency with the normal front running knee lift, such first attempts almost always terminate with the girl sliding along the floor, more or less unbecomingly, on her derriere. Fortunately, this is a very potent lesson, and players quickly learn to control the position of the hips in relation to the feet. Coaching emphasis on two points will speed this trial and error learning process: (1) In order to keep the center of gravity over the feet, the hips must not lead the feet as in front running. The torso actually is inclined forward (i.e., in the facing direction) from the waist, and the resulting body position gives the appearance of being quite erect. (2) The stride should feature a long reach and the floor contact should be on the toes and balls of the feet. As with all motor skills which involve unnatural movements, running backwards is best learned by running backwards. Minor style variations will appear, but the coach should be happy with a girl who can run backwards fast, whatever her form in getting the job done!

Stopping

A rather apparent corollary to any running technique is the ability to stop such motion. As in all footwork fundamentals, balance is again the key factor and in this particular technique, balance implies considerable skill in the rapid coordination of several essential actions.

The stop is normally associated with a dribble and is started by modifying the final running stride to a low-trajectory hop in which both feet touch down simultaneously. Although some players jump into a foot-planting stop, a sliding technique is more effective in controlling balance and is a much more difficult action for a defensive player to anticipate. The stop is properly executed as a sliding motion on the balls of both feet at the conclusion of a close-to-the-floor hop. Prior to the touchdown of the feet — during the hop phase of the maneuver — the center of gravity of the body is lowered and shifted to a location behind the feet by bending the knees and allowing the hips to drop downward and backward (see Fig. 4-3). Obviously, the greater the running speed at the time the stop is initiated, the greater will be the degree of this weight shift needed to counteract the forward motion of the runner. Actually, in the execution of the stop, a player goes through movements similar to those she would use if she were planning to sit down in mid-stride. As the counteraction of the stop takes effect, the hips again move forward shifting the center of gravity back over the feet as the athlete assumes the standard position of readiness.

Since most players favor one foot in front of the other in the ready position, this foot placement is the most commonly used form in stopping. It is usually described as the stride stop to distinguish it from a stop in which the feet are placed down parallel to each other, a form known as the *scoot* stop.

Pivoting

Pivots are turns made on the ball of one foot for the purpose of moving the basketball away from a defensive opponent. In general pivots have two chief aims — to provide increased protection for the ball, or to clear it for a more favorable shooting or passing position. Such maneuvers are essential offensive skills and the ability to execute effective back and front pivots, both to the right and the left, must be acquired early in the girl's playing career if she hopes to become an adequate performer in this sport.

A back pivot is a turn in which the initial free leg motion is toward the rear, and it is usually used by an offensive player in an attempt to place her body between the ball and the player guarding her. Such pivots are commonplace whenever and wherever a player with the ball is stopped and is being closely guarded in a face-to-face situation. Back pivots are classified as right or left depending upon the direction of the body rotation during the turn.

In making a back pivot to the right from a starting position of readiness, the player pushes off to the rear with the right foot, and pivots to the right on the ball of the left foot. As the turn is made, the right shoulder is lowered, the ball is moved with both hands to the right side of the body, and the right foot is placed down a full stride's length away from its original location in a direction away from the defensive player. The most important aspect of the back pivot is

FIGURE 4-3   Executing the stride stop. Note hip position and sliding action of feet.

the tactical use of the body as a screen between the ball and an opposing guard, and at the conclusion of whatever degree of turn is made in the pivot, the ball should be held waist-high in both hands in a position in which the body provides it with maximum protective coverage (see Fig. 4-4).

The front pivot is, by definition, a turn in which the free leg is moved forward, and as with the back pivot, it is designated a right or a left pivot depending upon the direction of the body turn. Front pivots are used primarily in the front court as a means of moving away from a player guarding from behind, in order that the offensive player may free herself momentarily for a one-handed shot or a more favorable passing situation.

When using the front pivot as a prelude to a shot, the action invariably begins with a step forward (that is, in a direction away from the defensive player behind the ball handler) onto the pivot foot.

FIGURE 4-4   Finish of back pivot to the right. Note ball protection and body balance.

In making a pivot to the left, the player steps forward from the position of readiness with her left foot, pushes off in a forward direction with her right foot, and turns to the left on the ball of her left foot. During the execution of the pivot, the basketball is moved into the appropriate shooting position.

When the front pivot is used to initiate a pass, the preliminary first step with the pivot foot is often omitted. If ball protection is the primary purpose, the ball is moved to the side of the body away from the guarding opponent at about waist height during the execution of the turn.

Individual Defensive Fundamentals

No matter how many team defensive alignments are developed, or what combinations of attention-getting names are attached to such team patterns, defense in basketball is basically an eyeball-to-eyeball confrontation between two individuals. Thus, when a player is in a defensive situation it is imperative that she assume a stance from which she will be able to react quickly and as adequately as possible to any conceivable offensive move made by her immediate adversary. The specific posture which allows this is called the basic defensive stance (see Fig. 4-5), and in assuming this position, the placement of the feet is the key to being able to move effectively. The feet must be spread comfortably, about hip width apart, with one foot slightly in front of the other. The knees are bent and the upper part of the body is inclined forward slightly from the waist. The arms are extended and the fingers of the hands are spread in an effort to offer maximum harassment to the player being guarded. One arm is held high; the other is at waist-level or lower. The high hand is held in the most favorable position from which to attempt to block or deflect most shots and passes and the low hand fulfills a similar purpose against possible low passes or the start of a dribble.

In order to maintain the essential ability to move rapidly in any direction, the feet must remain in the initial position of this basic stance whenever a defensive player is in a man-to-man situation against an opponent. This necessity requires the use of a boxer's shuffle for any changes of body location. The boxer's shuffle is a form of locomotion in which the lead foot (that is, the foot which moves first) is advanced a short step, and the trailing foot is then quickly brought to its original relative position. This technique is used irrespective of the direction of the body movement — forward, backward, or sideways. It is a serious defensive error for a player guarding in a one-on-one situation to take a forward or backward stride which brings one leg past the opposite one, or a lateral stride in which one leg crosses the other. These movements result in a momentary inability to move in one direction and experienced opponents will take immediate advantage of such errors.

In a very real sense the offensive player has an advantage. She knows what she plans to do — and when! For this reason, except when applying a press, experienced defensive players guard an assigned opponent loosely when such an adversary does not have possession of the ball, when she has the ball in a non-dangerous court position (for example, in the back court), or when the playing action is in an area of the court other than that occupied by the two antagonists. In situations like these the defensive player drops off, to the extent that she can do so and still maintain visual contact with her opponent, and bolsters the overall defense by such actions as clogging the middle or by providing a momentary double-team situation with a nearby teammate.

As any one of these situations changes so that the assigned offensive player becomes progressively more of a threat, the guarding athlete

FIGURE 4-5   Basic defensive stance.

must play her correspondingly tighter. When the play moves into a defensive player's zone of responsibility, or when her designated opponent gains possession of the ball in a scoring area, it is obvious that she must guard her opponent as closely as her skill will permit.

In general, the court position of each defensive player is determined by the team defensive pattern being employed. Individual players, however, are normally responsible for an assigned opponent or for any opponent in possession of the ball in a designated area of the court. This responsibility is of such a nature that experienced players on defense generally find it advisable to attempt to maintain a floor position which will meet three criteria at all times:

1. A position in which the defensive player is between her assigned opponent and the goal being defended.
2. A position in which the defensive player can keep her assigned opponent in view.
3. A position in which the defensive player can keep the ball in view.

Such a floor position can be envisioned as one point of a triangle in which the other two points are represented by the location of the ball and the location of the assigned opponent.

While this defensive triangle is a relatively straight-forward concept to understand and to walk-through in slow motion, making it work on a reflex-level in a game situation is a complex habit formation requiring long playing experience. In addition to a sound repertoire of fundamental defensive skills and an efficient peripheral vision, the ability to use the "eternal triangle" calls for an experience factor known as "basketball sense" — a continuous awareness of the total game situation plus the ability to anticipate the actions of both teammates and opponents.

Coaching Hints for Improving Footwork

1. Beginners at running backwards should practice at a slow pace. As body control increases, the tempo of the running should be picked up until the players can maintain balance while moving at top speed. Finally, a competitive element should be added by organizing backward running relay races among the squad members or by racing the girls against the clock in timed lengths or laps of the playing court.
2. Stopping is another footwork skill which must be learned initially at slow speed. Beginners can work well individually by dribbling four or five steps and then sliding into a stop before proceeding with a subsequent dribble. For this simple drill to be effective, the stop aspect must be emphasized. Most novices are so anxious to get on with the ensuing dribbling phase that the "stops" are merely pauses in which the center of gravity is never allowed to stabilize. The coach must

insist that the learners come to a complete stop of all forward motion after each dribble before proceeding. As the girls improve in technique, the pace may be increased to provide the players with learning experiences in judging the degree of weight shift needed to halt different running speeds.

3. Pivoting practice can be added to the forgoing drill by having the players make a back pivot followed by a pause and then a front pivot, at each stop.

4. A pivot and passing combination can be added by including a back pivot with a pass to a following runner, at a stop made upon hearing a whistle or vocal signal. Alternate the direction of turn.

5. The front pivot and shot combination can be practiced by having the player dribble from under the basket to the free throw line, stop, pivot, and shoot a one-handed shot. Alternate the direction of turn.

6. Moving in the fundamental defensive stance must be practiced until the technique of the boxer's shuffle becomes habitual. A very effective way of working on this skill is to scatter the squad over the court while the coach leads a drill in which she mixes calls for rapid changes in direction and stops. The players maintaining the defensive stance, move in response to the commands.

7. While the offensive player has a general advantage over her defensive rival, the latter does have one very important tactical advantage. As long as she maintains her position in the defensive triangle, she is *always* closer to the goal than her opponent. Except under circumstances in which an element of risk is tenable — and such judgment is acquired only through experience — players must habitually learn to stay between their assigned opponents and the goal they are guarding.

8. The defensive triangle concept is like insurance. A girl on defense cannot afford to disregard its imposed limitations unless (or until) she finds that she is either much faster or a much better player than her assigned opponent.

9. Some experienced players contend that it is best to watch the eyes of an offensive player with the ball; others recommend that the defensive player should watch the ball. The latter opinion is recommended for beginning or novice-class basketball players. Many athletes become very effective at faking with the eyes and feinting with other parts of their bodies. As far as the girl on defense is concerned, however, the important consideration is what is happening to the ball. If the guard is following the ball, the most clever eye shifts in the league won't have too much effect on her defensive reactions.

CHAPTER V

TEAM OFFENSE FOR THE
FIVE-PLAYER GAME

Offenses are of two general types: those employed against a man-to-man defense and those employed against a zone defense. A successful offensive team, of course, must also be prepared to meet the zone press or the man-to-man press.

Perhaps the most important general rule of thumb for the coach in regard to offensive play is to keep it as simple as possible. An offense which cannot be taught easily and quickly to a team will not see fruition in one season. The players must be able to react quickly and automatically as the various options of the offensive pattern develop. This can only be accomplished by keeping the offense simple and by constant drill on the options of the offense in use.

MAN-TO-MAN OFFENSE

Screen and Roll

The screen and roll is an effective two- or three-player offensive maneuver which can be developed into a complete offense against a man-to-man defense.

The basic purpose of the screen is to set a stationary block on one of the defensive players so that an offensive player is free to drive toward the goal or to stop and shoot from behind the screen (see Figs. 5-1 and 5-2).

The successful execution of this maneuver is dependent upon the player with the ball faking her defensive player toward the base line as the screener approaches, and then cutting as close to the screener as possible. Actually brushing the screener is recommended, leaving no room for the defensive player to cross in front of the screen. The

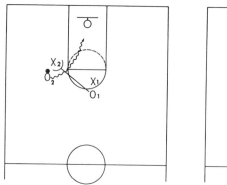 

FIGURE 5-1   FIGURE 5-2

player with the ball must be especially careful not to start her cut before the screen is completely stationary.

Most alert defensive teams will call for a switch of guarding players when one of the defenders is screened. When such a defensive switch is made, the screen and roll maneuver may be employed effectively by the offense.

To work a screen and roll successfully, the offensive players set the basic screen situation. When the switch is called by the defense (see Fig. 5-3), the screener (O_1) immediately pivots away from the guard she is screening (normally, this action will be a back pivot toward the inside) and cuts toward the goal. This action puts the defensive player behind her and gives O_1 a free path to the goal. Offensive player O_2 simply feeds the cutter a pass for an easy basket (see Fig. 5-4).

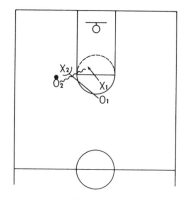 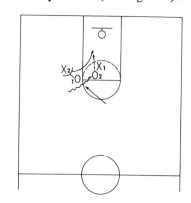

FIGURE 5-3   FIGURE 5-4

If a third defensive player tries to stop the cutter an offensive player must be open. If, for example, the pivot player's guard (X_4) tries to stop the cutter, it is a simple matter to give a quick pass to the pivot forward (see Fig. 5-5).

Screening away from the ball is another variation of the screen and roll. Instead of an offensive player setting a screen for the player with the ball, she sets a screen for a forward on the other side of the floor (O_3). This player sets up her defensive player for the screen by faking her guard toward the baseline and then cutting around the screen for a pass and easy goal (see Fig. 5-6).

When the screen is developed as a major part of the offense, the screening usually should take place on the side opposite the offensive pivot player (O_4) so as not to congest the area which is most vulnerable to scoring (see Fig. 5-7).

FIGURE 5-5

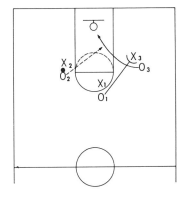

FIGURE 5-6

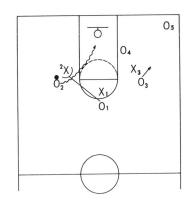

FIGURE 5-7

If the first screen and roll is stopped (that is, if the defensive player (X_2) is not effectively screened from her offensive opponent), it is a simple matter for the person with the ball (O_2) to move out from the congestion (see Fig. 5-8) and set another screen for one of the other forwards (see Fig. 5-9).

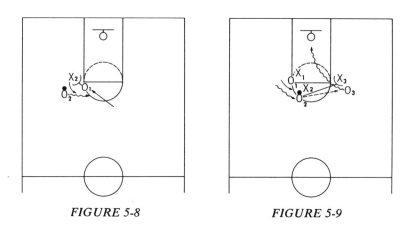

FIGURE 5-8   FIGURE 5-9

The pivot player may also be utilized to break out from the post position and set a screen for one of the forwards (see Fig. 5-10).

Any time a screen and roll is being attempted, the players not involved in the play must be extremely careful not to clog the scoring area by moving in too quickly for a rebound or a clearing pass (see Fig. 5-11). In doing so, they will move their guards into the scoring area and will defeat the purpose of the screen or the screen and roll maneuver.

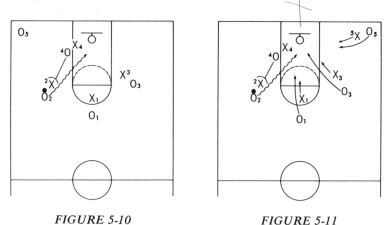

FIGURE 5-10   FIGURE 5-11

The well-coached offensive team which can move smoothly and repeatedly from one screening situation into another is inevitably going to spring a player free sooner or later. Such a team is hard to beat.

Split-the-Post

The split-the-post offense is used frequently when the offense has a tall girl playing the pivot or post position. It is really a simplified offensive series involving about four options. More options can be utilized but the basic four are usually sufficient to vary any offensive pattern.

In splitting the post, the pivot player (O_4) moves into a high-post position and the two nearest forwards, after passing the ball in to her, cut around the post in a scissors pattern (see Fig. 5-12).

The player who feeds the ball to the pivot makes the first cut, trying to screen her guard on the pivot player. The first quick move is usually initiated away from the intended cutting path to put the defensive guard in a position which makes her more vulnerable to being picked off (see Fig. 5-13). If this maneuver works, the pivot player will pass the ball back to the cutter as her guard is screened. For the maneuver to be successful, the cutting forward must pass as close to the pivot as possible to make certain that the guard cannot slide between her and the pivot player.

Immediately after the first forward starts her definite cut, the second forward fakes a cut away from her intended path and breaks around the other side of the pivot player for a pass (see Fig. 5-14).

If the defensive player guarding the pivot switches to pick up either cutter, the pivot player can turn and take a short jump shot or drive for the goal.

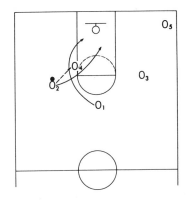

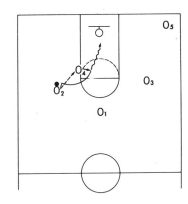

FIGURE 5-12   *FIGURE 5-13*

If the cutters have not been able to screen their opponents on the pivot player and none of the options are available, a clearing pass is made to O_3 (see Fig. 5-15). Often the player guarding the remaining forward will sag into the middle of the lane as she watches the play develop and this will leave her opponent open for an easy, medium-length shot.

FIGURE 5-14   FIGURE 5-15

High Post

This offense can be used successfully against a tight man-to-man defense. Usually it will be employed in the late stages of the game or when the defense is pressing.

The pivot player is stationed in front of the free throw line with the other players positioned away from the basket (see Fig. 5-16).

The pivot player does not necessarily have to be the usual offensive pivot player. In this situation the pivot player does not even have to be tall, but she must be a good driver and passer.

This offense depends on keeping the entire area from the free throw line to the basket open for drive-in shots. No shot except a lay-up is attempted. Thus, five good ball handlers who can drive are necessary for the effective execution of this offense.

The first option of the offense is to get the ball to the pivot player, in a one-on-one situation, and let her drive either way against her guard. The best position from which to get the ball to the pivot player is from the side, with the pivot player moving to that side to receive the pass (see Fig. 5-17).

If the pivot player starts to drive and cannot go in all the way for a shot, she stops and passes out to start the pattern over. It is important to remember that the one with the ball is not required to shoot and that only percentage shots are attempted.

The ball should never be forced in to the pivot position, but rather passed around and handled by the offensive players on the outside.

One of the most effective plays from this series occurs when the ball is passed in to the pivot from the side. Often the guard away from the ball (X_2) will focus her attention on the ball and momentarily lose

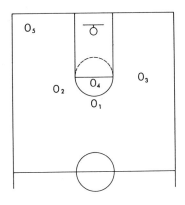

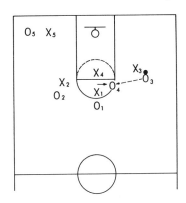

FIGURE 5-16   *FIGURE 5-17*

contact with her forward. In that split second, an alert forward can make a quick cut toward the goal and get a pass from the pivot player for an easy lay-up (see Fig. 5-18).

After this option is run several times on either side, the corner player (O_5) may often be broken loose for an easy goal by using the same maneuver with the cutter providing a moving screen for her. The corner player cuts immediately after the original cutter for a possible pass from the post player (see Fig. 5-19).

Frequently the defense will be putting so much pressure on the ball handlers that it is difficult to get the ball to the pivot, or even to one of

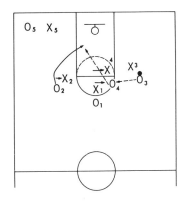

FIGURE 5-18   *FIGURE 5-19*

the other forwards. This can be remedied by two simple tactics — employing a great deal of interchanging of the outside players (see Fig. 5-20), and employing quick fake cuts toward the goal and coming back to get a pass (see Fig. 5-21).

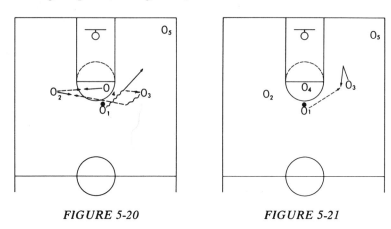

FIGURE 5-20   FIGURE 5-21

Double Post

The double post offense may be used effectively against both the zone and man-to-man defenses. Preferably, a double post is played with one player in a high post position (O_4) and the other in a low post (O_5) (see Fig. 5-22).

On the first option, the ball is fed to the high post player. She can turn and shoot or drive across the lane for a lay-up.

As the high post starts her cut the low post player (O_5) moves to the opposite side of the lane, clearing the area for her drive-in (see Fig. 5-23).

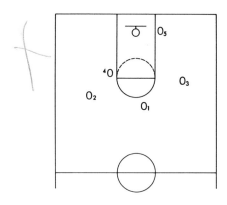 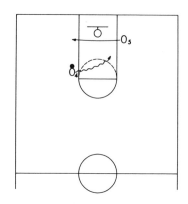

FIGURE 5-22   FIGURE 5-23

Frequently, the girl guarding the low post will try to help out against the cutting player, leaving the low post player open on the opposite side of the lane for an easy pass and score (see Fig. 5-24).

If one of the outside guards sags to help out the high post player, the post player passes the ball to the free outside girl and then receives a return pass as the guard moves back to her former position (see Fig. 5-25).

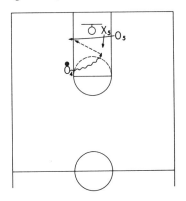

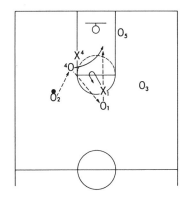

FIGURE 5-24   FIGURE 5-25

If the guard persists in sagging, the forward has an undefended medium shot with her teammates in good rebounding position (see Fig. 5-26).

If the double post is played side-by-side across the lane, it is a simple matter for the two offensive players to screen for each other (see Fig. 5-27).

All the screen and roll options previously discussed are available

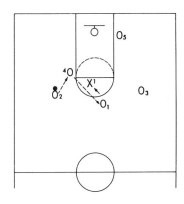

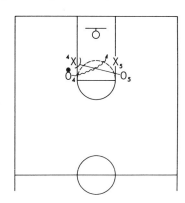

FIGURE 5-26   FIGURE 5-27

from this positioning. Also, it is a simple matter for one of the post players to move out and screen for the outside forward (see Fig. 5-28).

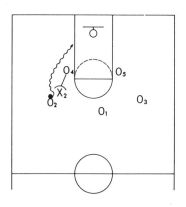

FIGURE 5-28

A resourceful coach can develop the double post to include the best features of the screen and roll, split-the-post, and a high-low post. It is only limited by the ingenuity of the coach and the players' ability and basketball sense.

Weave Offense

One of the most versatile man-to-man offenses is the simple weave. This is an offensive pattern which involves constant movement and screening to keep the defensive team off balance. The simplest option results from a "figure eight" maneuver with a resulting cut toward the goal for a basket (see Fig. 5-29).

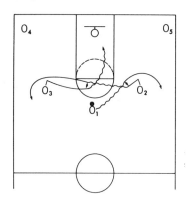

FIGURE 5-29

In utilizing the three-player weave, the player with the ball should always dribble on a diagonal rather than parallel with the end line. If this practice is not adhered to, the pattern will slowly move further and further from the basket.

After the weave has been run through completely once or twice, the defense will pick up the rhythm of the pattern and will be anticipating the offensive moves. In this situation player O_2 fakes a hand-off to player O_3, but keeps the ball and dribbles down the lane for a lay-up. This fake hand-off is accomplished by a simple change of pace or stutter step at the point the ball would ordinarily be handed off (see Fig. 5-30).

As the defensive team becomes aware of the front weave and fake weave, the offensive team should begin to utilize the corner players. A simple give-and-go can be implemented off the weave by having player O_3 make a quick pass to O_5 and cut to the goal for a return pass and score (see Fig. 5-31).

FIGURE 5-30

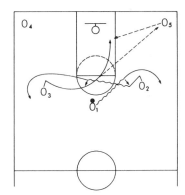

FIGURE 5-31

The weave can start either to the left or the right, but the front weave always must start with the ball in the middle. An alert offensive team will vary the starting direction of the weave to keep the defensive team off balance.

The weave offense can also incorporate a simple pick situation by having player O_1, after the first hand off, break the weave pattern and move to the corner to set a pick for player O_4 (see Fig. 5-32).

The weave can also be run on the side of the court utilizing the corner player. The two players away from the ball can also set a pick situation on their side of the floor (see Fig. 5-33).

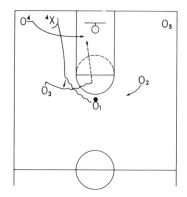

FIGURE 5-32   *FIGURE 5-33*

A simple split-the-post option can be implemented by having one of the corner players (O_4) break to a post position from which two outside players scissor around her (see Fig. 5-34).

One side of the floor can also be cleared for a potential score. The clear-out can be combined with a corner pick situation for a double option (see Fig. 5-35).

FIGURE 5-34   *FIGURE 5-35*

These are only a few of the possibilities which can be developed from a basic weave. Each of these options, of course, can be used on both sides of the floor with equal effectiveness.

OFFENSE AGAINST THE ZONE

In the zone defense each player is responsible for defending a given area of the floor in relationship to the position of the ball. This means that each player on the defensive team must shift position with every movement of the ball by the offense. Many of these shifts cover a great deal of floor territory and they must always be made as rapidly as possible. For a zone to be effective, the defense must be completely set before the offense attacks.

Rapid passing of the ball around the outside of the zone from one side of the court to the other, forcing the defensive team into repeated extensive shifts of position, is the basic principle of attack against these several defensive alignments. In theory, the offense should be able to move the ball faster than the defense can shift its entire team alignment in order to maintain the strength which is inherent in having five players defensively keyed on the ball. The quick pass around the periphery of the defense is an effort to gain an offensive advantage by getting the ball into an area of the court *before* the defensive players can set their most effective protective alignment for that particular ball position.

The most prevalent method of combatting the zone in present-day women's basketball is a combination of playing the gaps with one or two cutters creating an overload situation.

Offense Against the 2-1-2 Zone

In combating the 2-1-2 zone player O_1 initiates the attack by passing the ball to player O_4. At the same time, player O_5 moves toward the corner forcing the back defensive player (X_5) to go with her or to cover O_4. If she covers player O_4, player O_5 is open for a pass. The high post rolls down the lane into the area that X_5 must vacate in covering her zone responsibility (see Fig. 5-36).

If this option is stopped O_4 returns the ball quickly to player O_1 who immediately moves it to player O_2. After passing, player O_1 cuts through the lane toward the corner and player O_3 sets a high post on the lane.

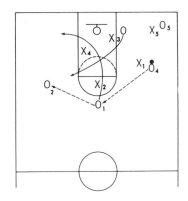

FIGURE 5-36   FIGURE 5-37

If player O_2 does not have an unhindered shot, either player O_1 or player O_3 should be in good position (see Fig. 5-37).

Moving the ball around the outside of the defensive alignment with short, snappy passes has always proved effective against a zone defense. If the quick passing is combined with a rotation of the high post player and the baseline player, the back of the defense can be overloaded.

With the ball in the center, a pass is made to O_4 forcing the zone to shift. Player O_4 returns it immediately to player O_1 who, in turn, passes it to O_2 on the opposite side of the court. Player O_2 dribbles toward the baseline. As the ball reaches player O_2, the high post player (O_3) rolls down the lane. This maneuver should put two players in the zone of the back defensive player on the ball side of the court (X_4). If the high post player is effectively covered, she cuts across the lane leaving the post position for player O_5. This clearing pattern frequently causes the defense to relax, and allows the player on the opposite side of the floor from the ball an opportunity to cut across the lane to receive a good pass (see Fig. 5-38).

FIGURE 5-38

If neither of the two front defensive players sag to keep the ball away from the high post, the ball should be passed to her as much as possible. If she is open she will often be in a good position for a pivot shot from the free throw line. If one of the outside players (X_2) sinks on the post player, the ball should be passed immediately to the wing player (O_2) on that side (see Fig. 5-39). The wing player should start a penetration with a dribble in order to make the back defensive player show. If this foil works, the baseline player immediately cuts into the area of the defensive player (X_4) who has challenged the player with the ball, and O_4 moves toward the baseline to pin down guard X_5. If defensive player X_4 does not challenge, O_2 will have an excellent scoring opportunity.

FIGURE 5-39

Offense Against the 1-2-2 Zone

One of the simplest patterns, similar to that used against the 2-1-2 defense, is initiated by feeding the ball to the post from the side. If front player X_3 picks up the post, the ball is quickly passed to the wing player (O_4) who must be covered by X_4, and the wing player on the opposite side cuts through the lane into the area vacated by the defensive player. At the same time, front player O_2 breaks toward the goal thus holding back defensive player X_5 in her zone, and creating several additional options (see Fig. 5-40).

If either back player moves up to guard the high post, both wing players cut for the goal, causing the other back player to defend against an overloaded zone (see Fig. 5-41).

The rotating pivots can be used to good advantage by getting the ball to the post player who immediately passes to a wing and cuts down the

FIGURE 5-40   *FIGURE 5-41*

lane. The back player on defense will have to pick up the post player, allowing the wing player on the opposite side to move across the lane and receive the ball in the high percentage area (see Fig. 5-42).

By moving the wing players into the deep corners and passing the ball to either of them, another simple option is revealed. As the ball moves to corner player O_5, the high post rolls down the lane picking back guard X_4, and the opposite corner player (O_4) cuts across the lane for a relatively easy pass and score (see Fig. 5-43).

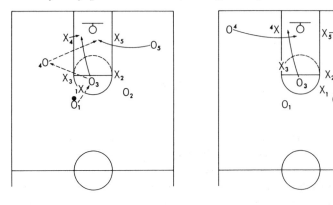

FIGURE 5-42   FIGURE 5-43

A simple overload option can be utilized by having an outside player (O_1) cut toward the corner as the corner player (O_5) cuts to the lane. Back player X_5 on that side must then commit herself to one player or the other. Further defensive confusion can be caused by having the post player cut down the lane to the opposite side of the floor (see Fig. 5-44).

FIGURE 5-44

Offense Against the 1-3-1 Zone

A high post pattern has proven to be effective against a 1-3-1 zone alignment. By passing the ball to corner player O_4, the back player on defense (X_5) is forced to cover that zone. A quick roll down the lane by the high post and a cut to the high post position by the outside player to hold X_3 at the foul line will often create beautiful confusion in the defensive assignments (see Fig. 5-45).

In a similar option, the ball is passed to the post by an outside player, moved quickly on to the other outside player, and finally passed into the corner. This rapid passing of the ball around the outside of the zone, forcing the defense into extensive shifting is the basic strategy in attacking a zone, and is a tactic which often will free the opposite corner player (O_4) to cut across the lane for a pass. In this situation, the post player should cut down the lane for an option-pass or to rebound (see Fig. 5-46).

FIGURE 5-45

FIGURE 5-46

A high post series which is very effective against the 1-3-1 zone can be implemented by a simple rotation of the post player and the two corner players as the ball is passed between the outside players. This rotation can be either clockwise or counter-clockwise. Changing the direction of the rotation will often create momentary confusion in a defense which has picked up the rhythm of the attacking pattern (see Fig. 5-47).

Another effective pattern for creating momentary confusion in the defense and overloading a zone is initiated with the high post playing slightly to one side of the free throw line. The ball is faked to one player opposite the ball (O_4) cuts across the lane, the outside player

the same time the high post cuts diagonally across the lane, the corner player opposite the ball (O_4) cuts across the lane, the outside player opposite the ball (O_1) cuts toward the baseline (see Fig. 5-48).

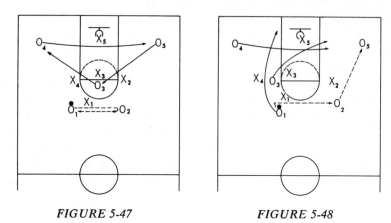

FIGURE 5-47   FIGURE 5-48

ALL-PURPOSE-OFFENSE

The revolving, or continuity, offense involves continuous motion with both man-to-man and zone options. The revolving offense uses a basic overload pattern from which all options begin (see Fig. 5-49).

By using the indicated overload, the offense has an advantage against the zone defense even before any of the basic options are run. The play begins by passing the ball around the outside to the corner player (O_4). Player O_3 then cuts toward the basket for a possible give-and-go option. If O_4 is open she shoots the ball. However, she also is aware of O_3 cutting for the goal. If the give-and-go does not develop, O_3 continues to the opposite side of the floor, O_4 moves out of the corner, clears the

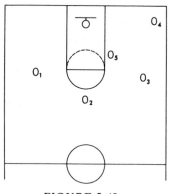

FIGURE 5-49   FIGURE 5-50

ball to O_2, and the pattern is repeated on the opposite side of the court (see Fig. 5-50).

As O_3 cuts toward the goal, O_5 attempts to screen her defensive player on the cut. If this is successful, she will receive a pass from O_4 (see Fig. 5-51).

If O_5 is not open for a pass, she continues to the other side of the lane and resets her post position there. During this action, O_4 clears the ball to O_2 at the top of the key (see Fig. 5-52).

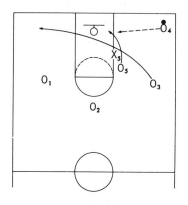

FIGURE 5-51

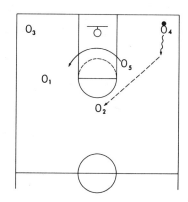

FIGURE 5-52

Immediately O_2 passes the ball to O_1. If this move is executed quickly, the zone will not be able to shift from the opposite side of the floor rapidly enough to keep O_1 from getting an unchallenged shot (see Fig. 5-53).

If the defense is able to cover O_1, O_3 or O_5 will frequently be open for a quick pass and score (see Fig. 5-54).

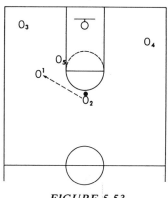

FIGURE 5-53

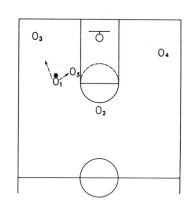

FIGURE 5-54

If neither O_1, O_3 or O_5 can get a good shot at the basket, O_1 makes a clearing pass to O_2, O_4 moves to the position originally occupied by O_3, and the offense is now in its initial alignment on the opposite side of the floor (see Fig. 5-55). The same set of options can now be run to the left side of the floor.

If the ball is passed to the pivot player (O_5), she is free to make a move to the middle or to the baseline. If neither option develops, she clears the ball to O_1. Player O_3 immediately breaks to a position on the lane adjacent to O_5 to set a double pick for O_4 (see Fig. 5-56).

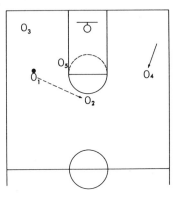

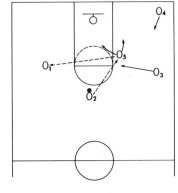

FIGURE 5-55   FIGURE 5-56

Now O_1 has the option of driving on her defensive player. If this does not develop, she picks up the dribble and clears back to O_2 who has covered the play by moving behind the ball. Player O_2 then passes the ball to O_4 breaking over the top of the double pick (see Fig. 5-57).

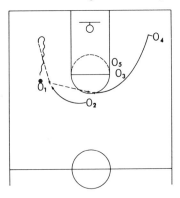

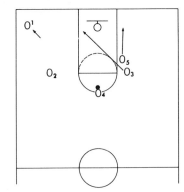

FIGURE 5-57   FIGURE 5-58

After O_4 cuts past the double pick, O_3 moves diagonally across the lane and O_5 moves down the lane. If O_4 does not have a clear shot, she looks for either O_3 or O_5 to be open (see Fig. 5-58).

If the pass to O_3 or O_5 does not develop, O_4 passes the ball to O_2 and receives it back as O_5 immediately breaks to the pivot position. Then O_3 attempts to screen her guard by cutting behind O_5, moving away from the basket. If either cutter is open, she receives the ball and the appropriate options are run. If neither player receives the ball, the original pattern has been re-formed (see Fig. 5-59).

If play is begun by a pass to the weak side, the weak side player tries to go one-on-one with the defensive player on that side of the floor (see Fig. 5-60).

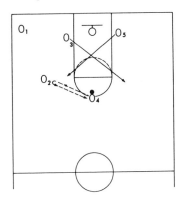

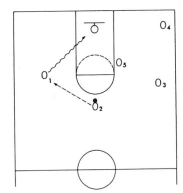

FIGURE 5-59   FIGURE 5-60

While O_1 is working on her guard, O_2 cuts through the lane to the opposite corner. Players O_3 and O_5 again set a double pick for O_4 who cuts across the top of the pick for a possible pass and shot. At the same time, O_3 cuts around O_5 and goes to the opposite side of the lane (see Fig. 5-61).

If O_4 is not given the pass, O_3 hesitates at the lane for a possible pass. At the same time, O_5 makes a "V" cut in and out of the lane. As O_5 emerges from the lane, O_3 continues her cut toward the corner. This move should create indecision in a zone defense. Taking advantage of this situation, O_2 leaves her corner position and moves to the area vacated by O_3 (see Fig. 5-62). If no one is open for a pass, the offense is back in the original overload position. The offense can then again begin any series of options. Each series, of course, is keyed by the direction of the first pass.

FIGURE 5-61   FIGURE 5-62

A real danger inherent in any revolving, or continuity, offense is the concentration of the players on pattern running. The players constantly must be reminded to look for the good shot. Many times scoring opportunities will be passed up because the players are so intent on running the patterns to their conclusion that they fail to keep aware of the developing playing situation.

OUT-OF-BOUNDS PLAYS

At many times during a game the offensive team will have the ball out of bounds in their scoring area. Using set out-of-bounds patterns, it is possible to score in such situations. The use of a large portion of practice time on these plays, however, cannot be justified, and as a general rule of thumb, all out-of-bounds plays should be kept as *simple* as possible.

In the five-player game the offensive team will never have the ball out of bounds beneath the goal at which they are shooting. Since all of the out-of-bounds balls in the scoring area will be taken at the side, the opportunities for easy baskets will be reduced.

The simplest maneuver to get the ball in bounds is to have the intended receiver make a short cut toward the basket, quickly pivot and return toward the ball. This maneuver will leave most guards standing since their first responsibility is to defend against the quick pass to the cutter.

When the ball is out of bounds on the side line in the offensive end of the court, a simple but effective set play employing a split-the-post concept can be employed. In this action, player O_3 breaks quickly toward the ball and receives it on the same side of the free throw lane as the out of bounds. Player O_1 immediately breaks behind O_3 — this is the first cutter past the pivot player (see Fig. 5-63). If the guard of O_1 is screened, the latter will receive a return pass from player O_3. An alert defensive team, however, will switch, or slide through, not allowing player O_1 to drive toward the goal. In this case, player O_1 simply continues across court in order to clear the side from which she started. Player O_2 makes a fake cut in the same direction as O_1, but then reverses to cut on the other side of the pivot player, takes a hand off, and drives toward the goal (see Fig. 5-64).

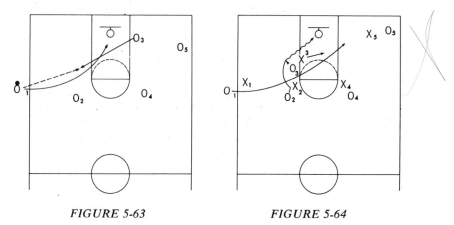

FIGURE 5-63   FIGURE 5-64

In the event that the pivot player's guard (X_3) drops off to defend against O_2, the pivot player can either take a short jump shot or drive to the goal (see Fig. 5-65).

FIGURE 5-65

During this action, players O_4 and O_5 should be running a simple interchange of position to keep their guards from sagging and disrupting the play.

Another simple out of bounds play can be utilized by aligning all five players on the same side of the floor, and using the screen and roll technique. In this pattern, player O_2 cuts toward the basket as if to receive a pass and then does a quick reverse back toward the ball to receive the inbounds pass. At the same time, player O_4 sets a pick on the player guarding O_5 and the latter, after making a feint toward the baseline, uses the pick to free herself in a cut toward the free throw line. Player O_2 attempts to get the ball to O_5 at this point (see Fig. 5-66).

Player O_4, after setting the pick, quickly rolls into the free throw lane for a possible screen and roll option. After inbounding the ball, player O_1 immediately cuts toward the goal along the baseline. If player O_5 does not have a shot from the free throw line, player O_4 may be free on the roll situation, or player O_1 may be free along the baseline. Usually the player guarding the out-of-bounds player will make some attempt to hinder, deflect, or intercept the inbounds pass. This activity will give the player inbounding the ball a half-step to a full-step lead on her guard if she will cut for the goal as soon as the ball leaves her hands (see Fig. 5-67).

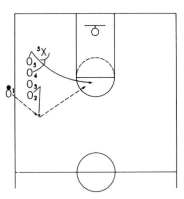

FIGURE 5-66	*FIGURE 5-67*

FAST BREAK

The fast break as a defensive weapon is perhaps the most underrated maneuver in basketball. No team that is psychologically tuned to drop back to defend against a potential fast break can effectively rebound to get that all important second and third shot at the basket. Any team with an effective fast break will see gratifying and immediate success on the defensive boards.

The success or failure of a fast break will depend upon the defensive rebounder getting clear possession of the ball and making a controlled clearing pass or dribble to move the ball from the congested area around the goal. If these two objectives can be accomplished smoothly and quickly, the ball can be moved into the scoring area with great efficiency. Obviously, the key element in the fast break is the rebounder. A good deal of the practice time devoted to the fast break should consist merely of the rebounder getting possession of the ball and moving it to the outside with a dribble or clearing pass. It will do well to have the rebounder practice both of these skills. Although the pass is quicker, frequently a long rebound will occur and the player gaining possession may be able to advance more rapidly up the floor by dribbling the ball.

The simplest fast break maneuver is the three-lane pattern in which the offensive team attempts to get the ball centered and to fill the right and left lanes with cutters towards the goal (see Fig. 5-68).

The fast break starts with the control of the rebound. The first, or clearing, pass is usually to the sideline in order to prevent a deflection in the congested middle area of the court. As the ball is rebounded, a guard or forward on the same side as the rebounder breaks to the sideline. At the same time the opposite guard breaks to the middle, and a third player attempts to fill in the lane opposite the ball (see Fig. 5-69).

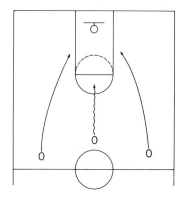

FIGURE 5-68

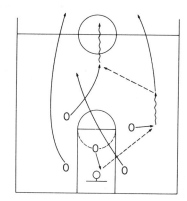

FIGURE 5-69

If the center player on the three-lane fast break does not receive the ball far enough downcourt, it may be necessary for her to pass to one of the lane players and to receive a return pass.

The player gaining the rebound will usually stay back as a safety man and the fifth player will become a trailer to the three-lane fast break.

The center girl should consider the free throw line as a barrier unless the middle is open for her to drive all the way for a lay-up. By stopping at the free throw line she puts more pressure on the defense. The center girl has two general options. She can shoot or pass to either teammate. A smart offensive player will try to draw one of the defensive players to her by faking a shot, and then hitting one of her teammates for an easy goal. A good jump shooter will be able to leap into the air and either attempt a shot or pass off as the guard commits herself.

After a team has run two or three successful fast breaks, the defensive guards will begin to lay back and wait for the break to develop. This puts a great deal of pressure on the center girl. *She is the key.* Through faking, she should attempt to draw one of the guards out of position. If possible, the center player must make the defensive player commit herself.

The defensive players commonly will play either side by side or in tandem. Either of these defenses can be beaten by the fast break since each is outnumbered three to two.

If the guards play side by side, the center player should be able to score at will. The center player simply stops at the free throw line and take an easy free throw shot.

When the defensive players position themselves deep in the lane, the side offensive players should not break all the way to the goal, but should stop about six feet from the lane for an easy pass and shot (see Fig. 5-70). If the defensive players position themselves in a high post position, the two side players should break all the way to the

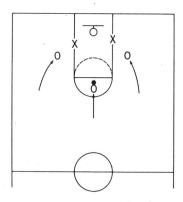   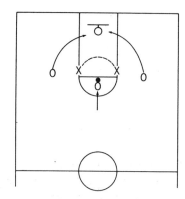

FIGURE 5-70   *FIGURE 5-71*

goal, because they will have room to slide behind the defensive players (see Fig. 5-71).

When the defensive players are in tandem, the center player must be certain that the front guard commits herself, and then pass off to either side player (see Fig. 5-72).

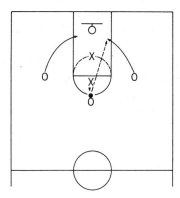

FIGURE 5-72

The best move for the defensive players to make from a tandem alignment is to have the low player (X_2) take the first pass and the front player (X_1) sag after the pass has been made (see Fig. 5-73). In this situation, a pass made across the lane to the other side girl (O_3) should be avoided as it is too vulnerable to being picked-off. The logical pass is a quick return to the center forward for an easy goal (see Fig. 5-74).

FIGURE 5-73   *FIGURE 5-74*

Drill on the three-lane fast break should be included in every practice session. It is not especially important which three players fill the lanes. The players who push themselves the hardest will usually be involved in most of the fast break situations. It is important that the three lanes are filled with no delay.

The coach should make sure that the players are aware of when the defense is crashing the boards and not looking for the fast break. In this situation it is relatively easy to get one player out in front for the long pass and the easy goal.

At times the defensive team will get three girls back on defense very quickly. In this situation the trailer becomes extremely important. If this player is hustling, the center player can veer to one side and drop the ball to the trailer creating a four-on-three situation (see Fig. 5-75).

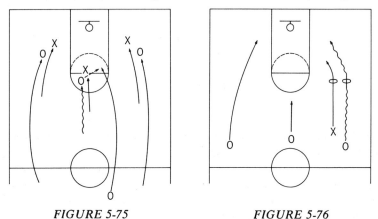

FIGURE 5-75   FIGURE 5-76

On some occasions, the offensive team will not be able to get the ball centered until they have advanced the ball well down the floor. The defense, however, probably will be looking for the ball to be centered, as most of the successful fast breaks are run in this manner. Since the defense is conditioned to such centering of the ball, it is often effective for the lane player with the ball to make a quick change of pace dribble at about the free throw line, looking toward the middle lane at the same time. This tactic will sometimes cause the defensive player to relax or take a quick glance toward the center lane. In either case, the player with the ball has gained the advantage and can continue toward the goal for a lay up (see Fig. 5-76).

CHAPTER VI

TEAM OFFENSE FOR THE TWO-COURT GAME

Offensive team play must be planned to attack both of the two basic defensive styles — the man-to-man defense and the zone defense. A successful offense must also be able to cope effectively with variations of these formations, especially the pressing defenses.

The key to sound offensive tactics is simplicity. Offenses should be of such a nature that they can be learned well in a short time. Every coach wants her players to learn the proper moves of each option to the degree that she will make them almost automatically as rapidly as the opportunities for such offensive choices develop during the course of a game. Such reflex-like responses will not be characteristic of the typical player unless the team offense is simple and unless drill on the various patterns is constant.

MAN-TO-MAN OFFENSE

Screen and Roll

A complete offense can be developed from the basic concept of this very effective two- or three-player tactic.

Basically, the screen is an attempt to block off a defensive player so that her opponent will be free to drive toward the goal or to stop and shoot from behind the protection of the screening teammate.

In making this maneuver the player with the ball attempts to fake her opponent toward the base line as the screen is being set, and then cuts as close to the screener as possible as soon as she is completely stationary. Actually brushing the screener is recommended procedure in order to prevent the defensive player from sliding through between the player with the ball and the screen.

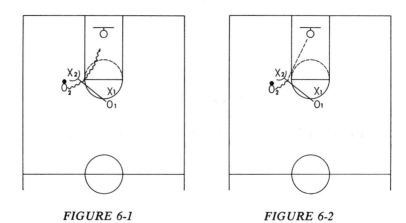

FIGURE 6-1   FIGURE 6-2

Normally, when defender is screened the defensive team will call for a switch of the guarding players involved in the maneuver. When such a change is made, the screen and roll may be employed effectively.

In executing the screen and roll, the offensive players set the basic screen and then when the defense calls for the switch (see Fig. 6-3), the screener (O_1) immediately pivots away from the guard she is screening and cuts toward the goal. This maneuver puts the defensive player behind her and gives O_1 an open path to the basket. A pass from O_2 should result in an easy score (see Fig. 6-4).

In this situation, a third defensive player will probably attempt to stop the cutter, but such a move will still leave an offensive player open. For example, if the pivot player's guard (X_4) moves to pick up

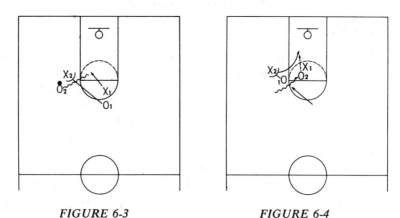

FIGURE 6-3   FIGURE 6-4

FIGURE 6-5

the cutter, a quick pass to the open pivot forward should result in an easy two points (see Fig. 6-5).

A frequently seen variation of the screen and roll is called screening away from the ball. In this maneuver, instead of setting a screen for the player with the ball, the screen is set for a forward (O_3) on the opposite side of the floor. The offensive player fakes toward the baseline as the screen is being set and cuts around the screen for a pass and easy goal (see Fig. 6-6).

If screening is used as a major part of the offense, the maneuver should normally take place on the side opposite the offensive pivot player (O_4) so as not to congest the scoring area (see Fig. 6-7).

Frequently, when employing the screen and roll, the defensive player (X_2) will not be effectively screened from her offensive opponent. In

FIGURE 6-6

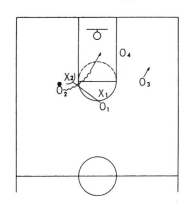

FIGURE 6-7

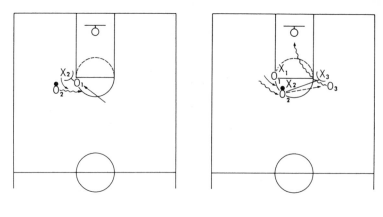

FIGURE 6-8   FIGURE 6-9

such a case the player with the ball (O_2) should move away from the congestion (see Fig. 6-8) and set another screen for one of the other forwards (see Fig. 6-9).

The pivot player may also break from the post position and set a screen for one of the forwards (see Fig. 6-10).

An important principle when attempting the screen and roll is that the offensive team members not involved in the play must not clog the scoring area by moving in too quickly for a rebound or clearing pass (see Fig. 6-11).

The ability of the offensive team to move continuously and smoothly from one screening situation to another is obviously an invaluable asset. Sooner or later such action will spring a player free and the team which can do this repeatedly is hard to beat.

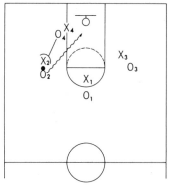

FIGURE 6-10   FIGURE 6-11

Split-the-Post

When the offensive team has a tall girl playing the pivot position, the split-the-post offense is very effective. This attack is basically a simple series in which about four options are usually sufficient to vary the pattern.

In executing the maneuver, the pivot player (O_4) moves to a high post position and the two nearest forwards cut around the post in a scissors pattern after the ball is fed to her (see Fig. 6-12). The first cut is made by the player (O_2) who feeds the ball to the pivot. She attempts to screen her guard on the pivot player. Normally, the first move of this cutter is away from the cutting path in order to set up the defensive guard in a more vulnerable position for a pick-off (see Fig. 6-13). If the cut is successful, the pivot player will return the pass to the cutter as her guard is screened. As with all screening moves, the cutting forward must brush the pivot player to make certain the guard cannot slide through.

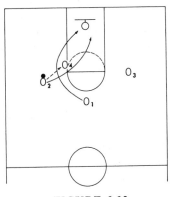

FIGURE 6-12

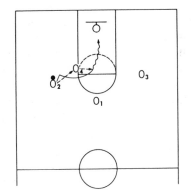

FIGURE 6-13

Immediately after the first forward begins her cut, the second forward fakes away from her intended path and breaks around the other side of the post for a pass (see Fig. 6-14).

If the pivot player's guard switches to pick up either cutter, she can turn and drive for the goal or take a jumper from the post position.

If the cutters have not been successful in screening their guards on the post player and none of the options are feasible, the ball is cleared to the remaining forward, O_3 (see Fig. 6-15). Often the player guarding O_3 will sag into the middle of the lane as the play develops, leaving the offensive player open for a relatively easy set shot.

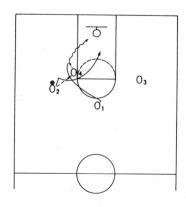

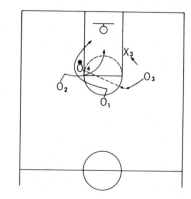

FIGURE 6-14   FIGURE 6-15

High Post

The high post is a very effective formation against a tight man-to-man defense. It is frequently used in the final few minutes of a game when the opponents are playing close to gain ball possession, or at any time when the defense is pressing. The high post gets its name from the position of the pivot player who stations herself in front of the free throw line. The other three players are positioned away from the basket (see Fig. 6-16).

In the high post offense, the pivot player does not have to be the usual offensive pivot. She does not even have to be tall but she must pass and drive well.

The underlying principle of the high post offense is that the area between the free throw line and the basket must be kept open for drive-in shots. No shots except lay-ups are attempted, so the effective

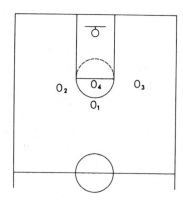

FIGURE 6-16

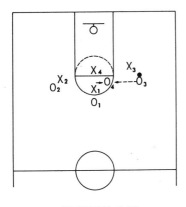

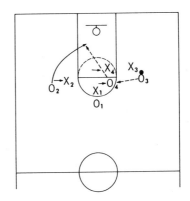

FIGURE 6-17   *FIGURE 6-18*

execution of this offense depends upon four good ball handlers who can drive well.

The initial option is to get the ball to the pivot player in a one-on-one situation and let her drive either way against her guard. The best way to get the ball to the post is by a pass from the side, with the pivot player moving to meet the ball in receiving the pass (see Fig. 6-17).

If the pivot player cannot drive all the way in, she stops and clears the ball to one of the outside players to start the pattern over. The player with the ball is never required to shoot. If a percentage shot is not available, the ball should be passed out. It should also be noted that the ball is never forced in to the pivot player. The ball should be passed around by the three outside players until the pass to the post becomes feasible.

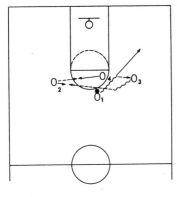

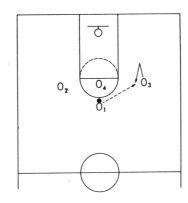

FIGURE 6-19   *FIGURE 6-20*

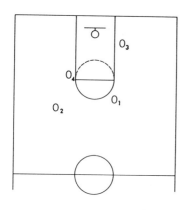 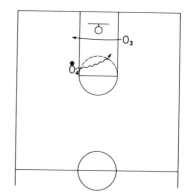

FIGURE 6-21   FIGURE 6-22

Often when the ball is passed in to the pivot from the side, the guard away from the ball (X_2) will turn her head to watch the ball and momentarily lose visual contact with the forward she is covering. An alert forward can take advantage of this situation by cutting for the goal and receiving a pass from the pivot player (see Fig. 6-18).

If the outside players have difficulty in getting the ball in to the post due to defensive pressure on the ball handler, interchanging of the forwards (see Fig. 6-19), combined with quick, fake cuts toward the goal and coming back to get a pass (see Fig. 6-20) is an effective remedy.

Double Post

The double post works well against either the man-to-man or the zone defense. Preferably, a double post is set up with one player in a high post position (O_4) and the other in a low post (O_3) (see Fig. 6-21).

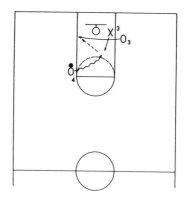

FIGURE 6-23

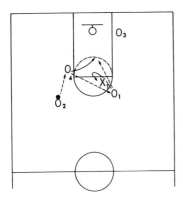

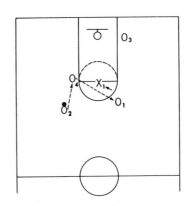

FIGURE 6-24   FIGURE 6-25

The first option is to feed the ball to the high post player who can turn and shoot or drive across the lane for a lay-up. In the latter situation, the low post player clears the area by moving to the opposite side of the lane as the high post begins her drive-in (see Fig. 6-22).

The guard covering the low post usually tries to help out against the cutting pivot player, and this may leave the low post open on the opposite side of the lane (see Fig. 6-23).

Sometimes one of the outside guards will sag to help out against the high post player. A quick pass from the post to the free outside girl will move the guard back to her original position and open the post for a quick return pass (see Fig. 6-24).

If the guard persists in sagging, the forward will have an undefended set shot with her teammates in good rebounding position (see Fig. 6-25).

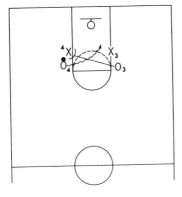

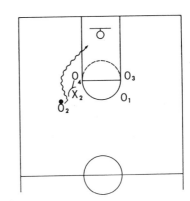

FIGURE 6-26   FIGURE 6-27

Many teams favor a double post played side-by-side across the lane since this is a formation ideally suited for the posts to screen for each other (see Fig. 6-26).

All of the screen and roll options previously considered are available with the side-by-side double post. Also, either of the post players are in excellent position to move out and screen for an outside forward (see Fig. 6-27).

A resourceful coach can develop the double post to include the best features of the screen and roll, split-the-post, and high post offenses. It is a most effective formation and is limited only by the ingenuity of the coach and ability of the players.

OFFENSE AGAINST THE ZONE

Each player in a zone defense has the responsibility of covering a specific area of the floor in relation to the position of the ball. With every movement of the ball each member of the zone must shift positions as rapidly as possible. Since many of these shifts cover considerable floor territory, offensive strategy is basically an attempt to move the ball around the outside of the defense, from one side of the court to the other, faster than the zone can be shifted to cover these moves. The strength of the zone is in having four players defensively keyed on the ball at all times. If the offense can move the ball into an area of the court before the defensive players can set their most effective protection alignment for that particular ball position, the offense will obviously have a distinct advantage.

The most effective method of combatting the zone is through the use of a combination of playing the gaps, with one or two cutters creating an overload situation.

Playing the Gaps Against the 1-2-1 Zone

Against a 1-2-1 or diamond defense, the offense should line up in a 2-1-1 offensive pattern with a high post (O_4) and a forward working the baseline (see Fig. 6-28).

In this type of alignment, the defense will either be forced into a man-to-man situation, or an offensive player will always be in an unguarded area.

With the ball on the right side of the court, X_2 will have to challenge the ball as it is moved toward the goal and X_1 will drop in front of the high post player (see Fig. 6-29).

If player O_3 on the baseline moves out toward the corner, X_4 must follow or she will be free to receive a pass for an unguarded shot (see Fig. 6-30).

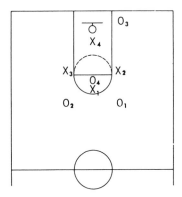

FIGURE 6-28

If X_4 follows player O_3 toward the corner, high post player O_4 can roll down the lane for a pass and a lay-up (see Fig. 6-31).

If X_2 does not challenge the ball, offensive player O_1 will have a medium length, unguarded shot (see Fig. 6-32).

Should X_1 challenge the ball, X_2 will have to cover the post player, X_4 will have to cover the baseline player, and X_3 will have to cover the other outside player forcing the zone into a man-to-man defense (see Fig. 6-33).

If X_4 covers the pivot player, X_2 will have to guard the baseline player, X_1 will have to challenge the ball, and X_3 will cover the other outside player. Again, the defense will be forced to change to a man-to-man situation (see Fig. 6-34).

These defense controlling maneuvers can be utilized with equal success on either side of the floor.

FIGURE 6-29

FIGURE 6-30

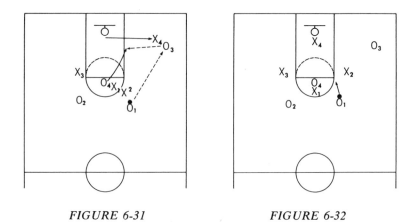

FIGURE 6-31   FIGURE 6-32

When a defense is forced into a man-to-man situation, any of the many screen and roll maneuvers can be used successfully against it, especially if the zone defense is the mainstay of the defensive team. Teams using the zone defense almost exclusively usually play a poor man-to-man when forced to depart from their zone defense.

Playing the Gaps Against the 2-2 Zone

Against a 2-2 zone, the offense will line up in a 1-2-1 formation, to put players in the natural gaps of the defense (see Fig. 6-35).

If X_1 challenges the ball, the point player on the offense will pass the ball to the forward on the side which X_1 was previously defending (see Fig. 6-36).

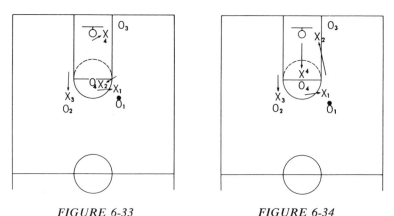

FIGURE 6-33   FIGURE 6-34

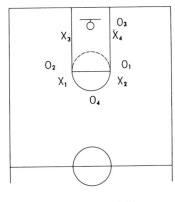

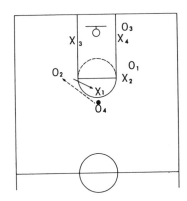

FIGURE 6-35   FIGURE 6-36

At the same time, offensive player O_3 on the baseline will cut across the lane to the ball side of the court. This requires defensive player X_3 to make the decision whether to challenge the ball or stay back to defend against the player nearest the basket (see Fig. 6-37).

If X_4 moves over to help out, the forward away from the ball (O_1) immediately cuts into the area thus vacated (see Fig. 6-38). These basic options, of course, can be worked on either side of the floor.

Frequently, if the point player on the offense is unchallenged, she can drive between the two front defensive players, X_1 and X_2, and score on a short jump shot in the lane.

If one of the second line of defensive players (X_3) moves to stop such a drive, the forward on that side should cut toward the goal for an easy basket (see Fig. 6-39).

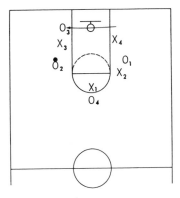

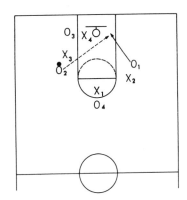

FIGURE 6-37   FIGURE 6-38

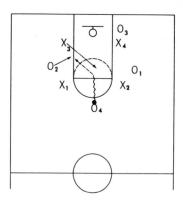

FIGURE 6-39

Overloading the Zone

The overload is used to flood one area of the zone, forcing the defense into errors or into a man-to-man situation. An overload situation may be achieved by using it as a set pattern or by breaking into an overload from a basic three out and one in pattern. If a team uses cuts to set up the overload, such maneuvers add options to those of the basic overload.

To start the overload, the offense lines up in a 1-2-1 pattern. The first cut is made by forward O_1 on the same side as the post player. If this first cutter is open for a pass, she is fed the ball for an easy score. If she is not open, she continues to the corner. The next cut across the lane is made by the pivot player, O_3. If she is open, she receives the ball and attempts to score (see Fig. 6-40).

If O_3 is not free, she remains on the opposite side of the lane thus creating an overload situation (see Fig. 6-41).

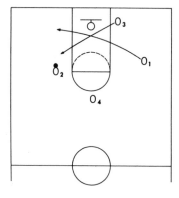

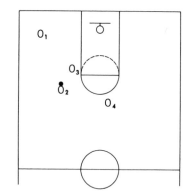

FIGURE 6-40   *FIGURE 6-41*

FIGURE 6-42

The offense now has several scoring options. If the defense insists on staying in a zone, the corner player will be open for a medium shot at will.

To effectively defend against the overload, the defense must convert into a modified man-to-man. If the corner girl is guarded, pivot player O_3 will frequently be in a one-on-one situation and should be able to score relatively easily (see Fig. 6-42).

If any defensive player sags to help out with the pivot player, one of the outside players on that side will have an unguarded medium shot (see Figs. 6-43 and 6-44).

With the overload situation, the outside player on the point (O_4) has a perfect one-on-one situation with one side of the floor cleared for a set-shot, drive and jump shot, or a drive in for a lay-up (see Fig. 6-45).

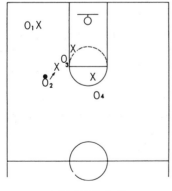

FIGURE 6-43

FIGURE 6-44

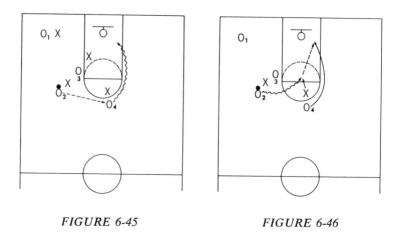

FIGURE 6-45   FIGURE 6-46

Another option occurs when forward O_2 starts to drive the lane, forcing the girl guarding the forward O_4 to either let her drive or to help out, thus freeing O_4 for a pass and easy score (See Fig. 6-46).

These cuts and options may be utilized on either side of the floor. As the game progresses, the defense will begin to anticipate the break into an overload, and will frequently ignore the first two cutters. *Obviously, this is the time to pass to the cutter.* It may get the one goal needed to win the game.

OUT-OF-BOUNDS PLAYS

At many points during the game the offensive team will have the ball out of bounds in their scoring area. Using set out-of-bounds patterns, it is possible to score in such situations. Out-of-bounds plays should be kept simple, however, since a large amount of practice time cannot be dedicated to these plays.

The simplest maneuver to get the ball in bounds is to have the intended receiver make a short cut toward the basket, quickly pivot and return toward the ball. This maneuver will leave most guards standing since their first responsibility is to defend against the quick pass to the cutter.

When the ball is out of bounds on the side line at the offensive end of the court, an effective set play employing a split-the-post concept can be employed. In this action, player O_3 breaks quickly toward the ball and receives it on the same side of the free throw lane as the out of bounds. Player O_1 immediately breaks hard and fast behind O_3 — this is the first cutter past the pivot player (see Fig. 6-47). If the guard of O_1 is screened, the latter will receive a return pass from player O_3.

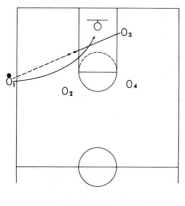 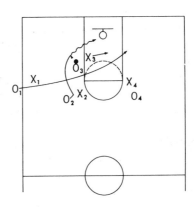

FIGURE 6-47   FIGURE 6-48

An alert defensive team, however, will switch or slide through, not allowing player O_1 to drive toward the goal. In this case, player O_1 simply continues across court in order to clear the side from which she started. Player O_2 makes a fake cut in the same direction as O_1, then reverses to cut on the other side of the pivot player, takes a hand off, and drives toward the goal (see Fig. 6-48).

If the pivot player's guard (X_3) drops off to defend against O_2, the pivot player can take either a short jump shot or drive to the goal (see Fig. 6-49).

Player O_4 should also be making a move wide to her right to keep her guard from sagging and disrupting the play. She will then be in a better position to defend against the fast break if the set-play is stopped.

One or two baskets a game can usually be made from situations in which the ball is out of bounds beneath the offensive team's basket. It is

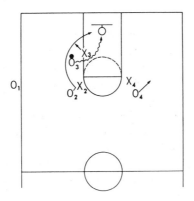

FIGURE 6-49

not good percentage basketball to plan on more out-of-bounds scoring plays unless an exceptionally weak opponent is being played. In a tight game, however, one basket may spell the difference between victory and defeat.

One of the simplest out-of-bounds plays involves a formation in which the offensive players line up in file along the free throw lane facing the player making the throw-in. If the defensive team is watching for a break to the basket for an easy goal, the guarding players will normally line up in a formation to prevent this — and actually they have no logical choice except these inside positions (see Fig. 6-50). Upon a signal by the out-of-bounds player, such as bouncing the ball or slapping it, offensive player O_1 becomes the post, O_2 breaks to the outside, and O_3 breaks to the opposite side (see Fig. 6-51). Although in action this play seems completely unorganized, the moves are keyed to the defensive alignment. By cutting to the left, player O_2 screens her guard, X_2, on the post player (O_1) for an easy shot close to the goal.

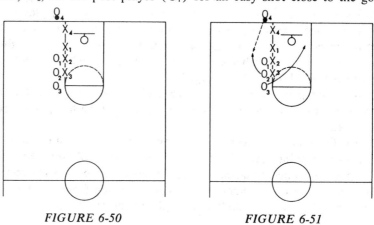

FIGURE 6-50   FIGURE 6-51

The tighter the defense plays their man-to-man, the easier it will be to free a player momentarily for a quick score.

Player O_1 may chose to break to the left taking her guard with her, while player O_2 cuts across the lane, and player O_3 cuts down the lane toward the baseline (see Fig. 6-52).

This set-play, obviously, has unlimited variations. The apparent confusion covering a simple screening situation is the key factor, and the imagination of the offensive players is the only limitation.

Another, perhaps even simpler, out-of-bounds play is started with the players lined up at the free throw line parallel to the baseline (see Fig. 6-53).

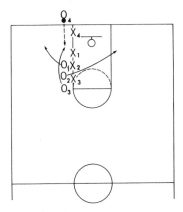

FIGURE 6-52

Player O_3 cuts behind players O_1 and O_2. If her guard drops off in an attempt to pick her up as she comes from behind the screen, she stops behind the double screen for a pass and relatively easy medium shot (see Fig. 6-54).

If guard X_3 should follow her, she will be open for a pass and an easy drive in (see Fig. 6-55).

The logical defensive move in this situation if for the outside defensive player on the side the cutter is moving toward, to switch and pick her up. However, if this switch is made, the offensive player whose guard has left her to make the switch, cuts directly for the goal for an easy basket (see Fig. 6-56). Even if the defense is very clever at switching, one offensive player should be open for a cut to the goal.

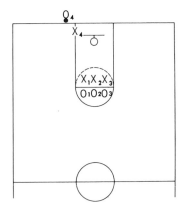

FIGURE 6-53

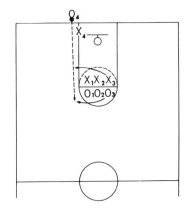

FIGURE 6-54

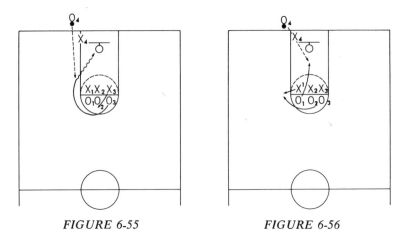

FIGURE 6-55   FIGURE 6-56

FAST BREAK

Owing to the nature of the girl's game with the roving player the fast break situation will usually develop into a three-on-two or a four-on-three situation. It is very rare indeed that a two-on-one pattern will develop and it would not be feasible to practice such a situation.

The sucess or failure of a fast break will depend upon the defensive rebounder getting clear possession of the ball and making a controlled clearing pass or dribble to move the ball from the congested area around the goal. If these two objectives can be accomplished, the ball can be moved into the scoring area with great efficiency. The rebounder becomes the key element in the fast break. A good deal of the practice time devoted to the fast break should consist merely of the rebounder getting possession of the ball and moving it to the outside with a dribble or clearing pass. A rebounder should practice these skills since frequently

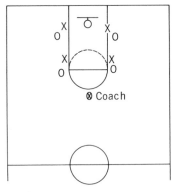

FIGURE 6-57

she will be the rover and will be responsible for advancing the ball by herself.

A good rule of thumb to follow is to have the stationary rebounder always give an outlet pass to the rover and let the rover-rebounder dribble the ball up the floor.

An effective drill is to have the coach stand at the perimeter of the scoring area and shoot at the basket, with both teams attempting to rebound the ball (see Fig. 6-57).

This drill serves as a general rebounding drill as well as a practice in initiating of the fast break.

Three-Lane Fast Break

The three-lane fast break is the simplest of the fast break maneuvers to execute and teach. It consists of advancing the ball down the court as quickly as possible and getting one of the offensive roving players into the forward court before one of the defensive rovers can get back, thus creating a three-on-two situation. A two-on-two situation automatically exists and it is very simple to get the three-on-two if the break is well controlled.

After a shot, the defensive players rebound and move the ball by dribbling or passing to a rover. The rover with the ball moves it up the floor by passing to a stationary forward who comes toward the center line to receive the pass. *This is a critical point of the fast break.* The stationary forward must be stationed at least 20 to 25 feet from the center line and in about 8 to 10 feet from the side line. These stationary forwards move in a diagonal line to the center division to receive the pass (see Fig. 6-58). The pass from the rover to a forward must be to the side away from the defensive player covering that forward. If the forwards are positioned too close to the center line or do not move in a

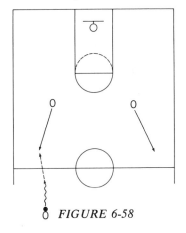

FIGURE 6-58

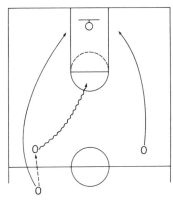

FIGURE 6-59

diagonal line to receive the pass, they leave themselves at the mercy of a smart guard. All the guard has to do is to step across the center line in front of the stationary forward, and either slap the pass away or be guilty of a violation. In either case the fast break will be stopped.

The first option of the forward who receives the pass is to pivot and dribble to the foul line and stop. The rover who has made the pass continues up the same side of the floor. The opposite stationary forward, who also has come to the line to receive a pass, wheels and heads for the goal on the opposite side of the floor (see Fig. 6-59).

The three lanes have now been formed with the girl in the center having possession of the ball. The next move depends on the defensive alignment. The center girl has two general options. She can shoot or pass to either teammate. A smart forward will try to draw one of the guards to her by faking a shot and then hitting one of her teammates for an easy goal. A good jump shooter will be able to leap into the air and either attempt a shot or pass off as the guard commits herself.

As the fast break develops, a guard may play off the forward coming to meet the pass. After receiving the pass, this forward can return pass to the rover down the middle, and fill in the lane on the side she normally plays. The rover is now the forward in the center of the three lanes (see Fig. 6-60).

The same situation will develop if the forward on the same side of of the rover is covered by her guard. The rover can pass to the forward on the opposite side and get the return pass down the middle (see Fig. 6-61).

Frequently, when the forward is being guarded closely by an over-anxious defensive player, she can move toward the center line, letting the guard stay right on her shoulder. Then, with a simple pivot and cut

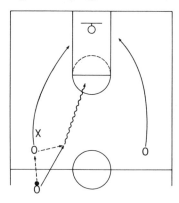

FIGURE 6-60

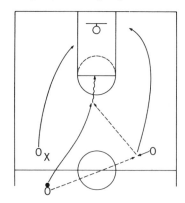

FIGURE 6-61

FIGURE 6-62

toward the goal, she can leave the guard standing and be free to receive a lob pass for an easy lay-up. This can be a very effective move if the rover will fake a pass to the forward at the center line causing the guard to commit herself (see Fig. 6-62).

After a team has run two or three successful fast breaks, the defensive guards will begin to lay back and wait for the break to develop. This puts a great deal of pressure on the center girl. *She is the key.* Through faking she should attempt to draw one of the guards out of position. If possible, the center player must make the defensive player commit herself.

The defensive players will usually play either side by side or in tandem. Either of these defenses can be beaten since they are outnumbered three to two.

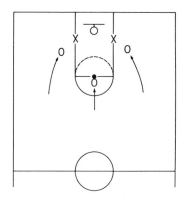

FIGURE 6-63

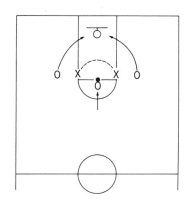

FIGURE 6-64

If the guards play side by side the center player should be able to score at will. The center player must stop at the free throw line and take all the time she needs to sink the goal.

When the defensive players position themselves deep in the lane, the side offensive players should not break all the way to the goal, but should stop about six feet from the lane for an easy pass and shot (see Fig. 6-63). If the defensive players position themselves in a high post position, the two side players should break all the way to the goal because they will then have room to slide behind the defensive players (see Fig. 6-64).

When the defensive players are in tandem, the center player must be certain that the front player commits herself and then pass off to either side player (see Fig. 6-65).

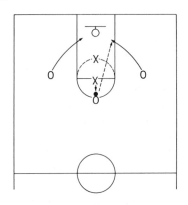

FIGURE 6-65

The best move for the defensive players to make from a tandem alignment is to have the low player (X_2) take the first pass and the front player (X_1) sag after the pass has been made (see Fig. 6-66). In this situation a pass made across the lane to the other side girl (O_3) should be avoided as it is too vulnerable to being picked-off. The logical pass is a quick return to the center forward for an easy goal (see Fig. 6-67).

Four-on-Three Fast Break

The four-on-three fast break is essentially a delayed fast break. This maneuver was perfected by the Nashville Business College team. The pattern is based on both roving players becoming potential scorers on the break.

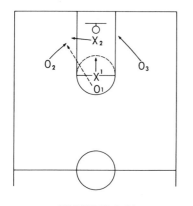

FIGURE 6-66   FIGURE 6-67

After the defensive player has rebounded and the ball is being advanced up the floor, both stationary forwards break to the center line. These forwards are stationed initially in the same position as they were during the three-lane fast break. The forward on the same side as the ball is advancing breaks to that side. The opposite forward breaks to the line at the center of the court (see Fig. 6-68).

The first option is to pass the ball to the forward nearest the ball. The forward pivots and passes to the opposite forward, who had cut toward the free throw line when it was evident that she was not going to receive the initial pass. The stationary forward with the ball hits her with a pass at the top of the key and she then has the option of stopping at the free throw line or going all the way to the goal if she has her defensive player beaten (see Fig. 6-69).

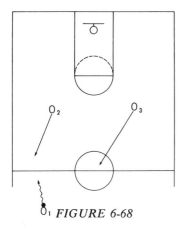

FIGURE 6-68

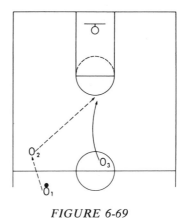

FIGURE 6-69

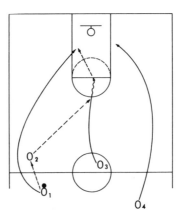

FIGURE 6-70

The roving player who is coming up the side from which the pass crossed the center line, continues up the floor and fills in the lane on that side. She is now in a position to receive a pass from the center girl for a lay-up (see Fig. 6-70). The roving player on the side opposite the ball delays until the rover on the side of the pass crosses the center line and she then fills in the opposite lane.

The *delay* is the key to this type of break. Instead of three lanes being filled, the girl in the center will be the first prong of the attack, the rover on the side from which the ball crossed the division line will be the second threat, and the rover opposite the ball will be the third scoring threat.

Again, the girl in the middle controls the situation. She may shoot from the free throw line or pass off to either of the cutting players.

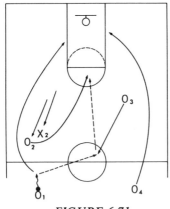

FIGURE 6-71

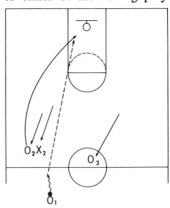

FIGURE 6-72

If the stationary forward coming to meet the pass is closely guarded, the ball is passed to the stationary forward coming to the center of the court. The opposite stationary now cuts to the middle and receives the pass to become the center player (see Fig. 6-71).

Either stationary forward, if closely guarded, may pivot and head for the goal to get a high lob pass for an easy basket. The rover bringing the ball up the floor usually keys this play by stopping and faking a pass to the stationary forward at the center line (see Fig. 6-72).

CHAPTER VII

TEAM DEFENSE FOR THE FIVE-PLAYER GAME

MAN-TO-MAN DEFENSE

The man-to-man defense will, in most cases, be the "bread and butter" defense of winning teams. In addition to learning the basic individual fundamentals of defense, a team must be imbued with the team play concept of this defensive formation in order to employ it most effectively.

In the basic man-to-man defensive alignment, the defensive players closest to the ball should always be putting pressure on their respective opponents and players away from the ball should be sagging (see Fig. 7-1).

This concept is perhaps the most important aspect of the man-to-man defense. Often one will see a defensive player (X_2) lose her offensive opponent who then will drive right by another defensive

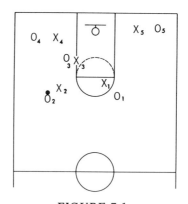

FIGURE 7-1

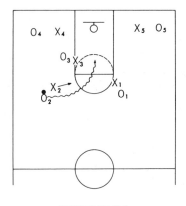 

FIGURE 7-2   FIGURE 7-3

player *not even aware* that she is in a position to help out (see Fig. 7-2).
If in this situation player X_1 had been sagging, she could easily have
stopped the opposing player from scoring. By sagging she may even
have discouraged the offensive player from attempting a drive-in (see
Fig. 7-3).

After losing her offensive opponent, player X_2 should immediately
drop back to the middle of the lane, *and then* look for the player who
is loose as a result of the switch made by X_1 to stop her player (see
Fig. 7-4).

Players X_3, X_4, and X_5 should be alert for a possible pass to their
players. However, within scoring range the person with the ball must
be stopped before the defense starts worrying about a possible pass-off.
Remember: *Only the player with the ball can score!* Often a team will

FIGURE 7-4

have all the potential passes defensed, but the person with the ball shoots and scores. Whenever a decision has to be made, the defense must go after the person with the ball even though it means leaving a potential scorer open. The pass to the open person may be deflected or badly thrown. An extra pass always leaves room for an extra mistake.

Many teams use an offense utilizing screening. A man-to-man defense is especially vulnerable to this type of strategy. Whenever a player is screened, the closest defensive player should call out "switch!" if it is clear that the defensive player cannot slide through the screen. The defensive player calling the switch now picks up the offensive player of the girl who was screened, and the girl screened guards the offensive player of the girl who called the switch (see Figs. 7-5 and 7-6).

If the offensive players change position or cross-over, the defensive player guarding the person with the ball should slide through between the other refensive player and her offensive player (see Fig. 7-7). She

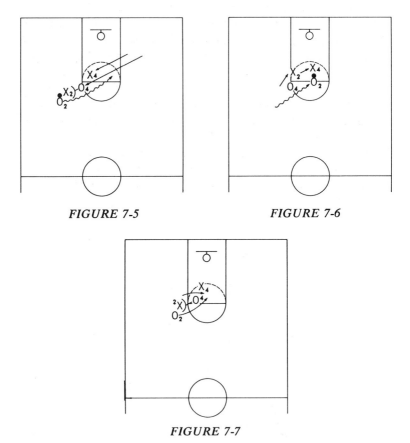

FIGURE 7-5   FIGURE 7-6

FIGURE 7-7

should never cross behind her teammate as this allows her opponent time to get set for a shot.

The defensive player should not react to the maneuvers of the offensive player. Usually, right handed players prefer to dribble and drive to the right. An alert defensive player will overplay the offensive player showing this tendency, a half step in that direction. This will tend to force the offensive player to drive only to her left. The defensive player, knowing the most likely move of the offensive player, can easily adjust to this maneuver and be ready to shift to the left to force the driving player wide.

Defending the Post Player

If the offensive team has a high-scoring pivot player, the ball must be kept from her. Any good pivot player, upon receiving the ball in or around the free throw lane, will score or draw a foul. Thus it is imperative to make it as difficult as possible for the pivot player to receive the ball. The defensive player assigned to the post player should position herself between the post and the ball to the extent that she can do so without giving the post player an untenable advantage on a possible break toward the goal (see Fig. 7-8). The degree of risk which the defensive player can afford to take in keeping in front of the post player will depend primarily upon the relative difference in playing ability between the two opponents.

The defensive player guarding the person with the ball must do one of two things: (1) Sag off the person with the ball if she is a poor long-shot, making it difficult for her to get the ball in to the pivot-player (see Fig. 7-9); or (2) Play the person with the ball very tightly if she has a good long-shot, attempting to force her to make a

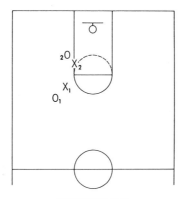

FIGURE 7-8

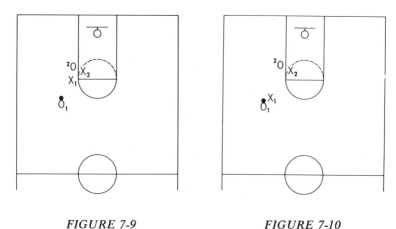

FIGURE 7-9   *FIGURE 7-10*

hurried, and perhaps poorly thrown, pass to the post player (see Fig. 7-10).

The remaining three defensive players should be alert to sag in case of a high lob pass behind the defending player to the pivot for an easy basket (see Fig. 7-11).

ZONE DEFENSES

A zone defense, well-played, is the strongest rebounding defense that a team can employ. A successful zone depends upon quick-moving, ever-alert players who refuse to let up. It is a physically demanding effort, but one which can demoralize any offensive team that is not having an exceptional shooting night from the field.

FIGURE 7-11

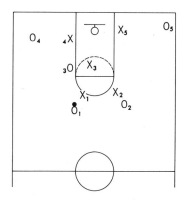

FIGURE 7-12

Effective zone play depends on many factors such as keeping the hands up, talking among the defensive players, and *always* keeping the feet pointed toward the ball. Zone defense is ball-oriented. Being ball-oriented, the ideal position for all defensive players is to be facing the ball at all times. This position allows for easy lateral movements as well as advancing and retreating motions.

2-1-2 Zone Defense

The 2-1-2 defense employs two front players, two back players, and a middle player (see Fig. 7-12).

As the ball moves to the corner, X_4 has corner responsibility, X_3 moves down the lane to protect against a pass to the post player or a

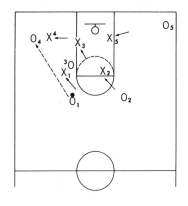

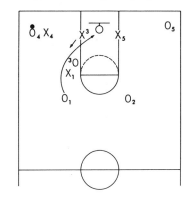

FIGURE 7-13   *FIGURE 7-14*

possible cutter, X_1 sags toward the goal to prevent an easy pass to the high post player or a possible cutter, and X_2 moves to the middle of the free throw line. X_1 also must be ready to challenge a possible return pass to the back offensive player, (O_1) (see Fig. 7-13).

Both back defensive players, X_4 and X_5, have corner responsibilities, and X_3 must assume the responsibility of defending a low post player or preventing a pass to a player cutting down the lane area (see Fig. 7-14).

1-2-2 Zone Defense

The 1-2-2 defense involves a point player and box (see Fig. 7-15). As the ball moves, the player nearest the ball becomes the point, and the other players form a box behind her. As the ball moves to the corner, X_5 becomes the new point player on the ball, the other back

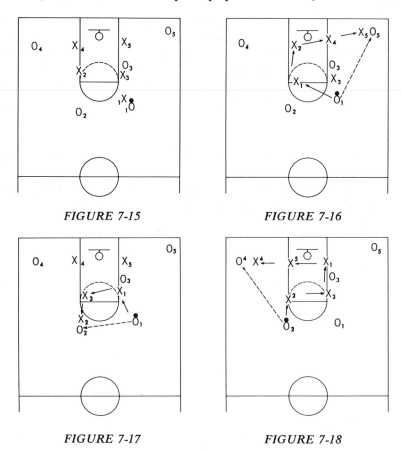

FIGURE 7-15　　　　　　　　　FIGURE 7-16

FIGURE 7-17　　　　　　　　　FIGURE 7-18

player, X_4, moves across the lane, X_2 moves down the lane to become a back player, and X_1, the original point player, drops back to fill the gap left by X_2 (see Fig. 7-16).

If the ball moves to the other side, X_2 becomes the point player, X_3 replaces X_2 in the box, and X_1 drops into the spot vacated by X_3 (see Fig. 7-17).

If the ball continues into the corner, X_4 moves toward the corner, X_5 comes across the lane, X_2 drops back to her original position, X_3 regains her original position, and X_1 moves down the lane beneath the goal (see Fig. 7-18).

1-3-1 Zone Defense

The 1-3-1 defense is a diamond shaped defense with a player in the middle of the key (see Fig. 7-19).

The middle player on the defense, X_3, should be the strongest rebounder. Player X_5 should be very quick as it is necessary for her to cover both corners.

As the ball comes up the floor, the point player (X_1) attempts to herd the ball to one side. At this time X_2 should attempt to make the offensive player pick up her dribble, and if successful, will either drop off to cover the possible pass to O_2, or will effect a double team on the player with the ball. X_3 will drop back to defend the pivot player, X_5 will come across the lane in readiness to move to the corner if the ball goes to that zone. Dropping back a little, X_4 will defend against the possible cut-through or a cross court pass (see Fig. 7-20).

It is very important for the point player (X_1) to herd the ball toward the sideline. The offensive team will not be so likely to catch the back

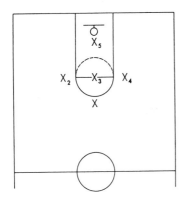

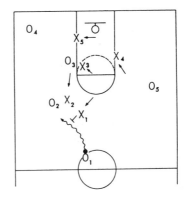

FIGURE 7-19   FIGURE 7-20

player (X_5) out of position if play can be limited to one side of the floor. With the ball moved to the side, the point player should harrass the ball handler and attempt to cut off the cross court passing lane.

As the ball moves to the corner, the back player (X_5) moves to cover this zone, the wing player on the side of the ball (X_2), attempts to cut off a return pass to O_2, the point player (X_1) drops back toward the middle to prevent a long clearing pass to the back court, the middle player (X_3) drops down the lane to defend against a possible pass to the post player or to a cutter, and the wing player opposite the ball (X_4) becomes the back player away from the ball (see Fig. 7-21).

FIGURE 7-21

COMBINATION DEFENSES

Combination defenses are those defenses which utilize zone-type play by some of the defensive team and man-to-man defense by other members. In the transition from the four-player game to the five-player game, it might be well to consider the possibilities of utilizing combination defenses. Many women's teams presently are playing either a diamond zone or box defense. It is a simple matter to align a team in its present zone defense and use the fifth player in a man-to-man role where strength is needed in relation to the strengths of the opposition.

If the offensive team has an exceptionally capable post player, it might be advisable to employ a player inside the typical four-player zone whose specific assignment is to defend man-to-man against the pivot player. Within the confines of a diamond defense, this combination defense would look very much like the 1-3-1 zone previously considered (see Fig. 7-19).

If the opposition has an especially strong outside player, one defensive player could be assigned to guard her. This concept, used with a box zone, gives the appearance of the 1-2-2 zone defense. Such a defense could be adjusted so that any opponent might be defended on a man-to-man basis, with the rest of the team employing their usual four-player zone.

One of the most effective combinations is to use the front players in a man-to-man situation, with the back players zoning. This pattern is sometimes reversed, with the front players zoning and the back players defending in a man-to-man alignment.

DEFENDING AGAINST THE FAST BREAK

Some opponents will employ a good fast breaking game and much emphasis must be placed upon stopping or rendering this offense less effective. In general, strong rebounding is the best defense against a fast break. If there is no possibility of gaining the rebound, the defense should attempt to deflect the ball out of bounds. If this tactic does not work, the successful rebounders should be harrassed as soon as she takes the ball off the boards in order that she will not be able to make the quick outlet or clearing pass essential in initiating the fast break.

Most good fast breaking teams have definite spots to which they throw an outlet to begin the fast break. If these can be identified through scouting, alert defensive players should be able to make a few timely interceptions or deflections, which will make the offensive team more conservative in their passing — and thus less effective.

If the offensive team makes the good outlet pass, it is imperative that the guards retreat immediately to a tandem position beneath their goal (see Fig. 7-22).

The front defensive player, X_1, attempts to stop the advance of the ball. As the ball is passed to the side, X_2 defends against the player

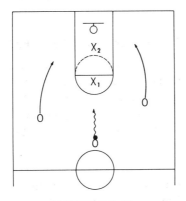

FIGURE 7-22

to whom the ball is passed, and X_1 drops to a position in the middle of the lane to prevent a cross court pass (see Fig. 7-23).

If a pass is made back to the middle, X_1 will move up the lane and X_2 will move back to her original position. Hopefully, by this time help will be coming from the back court (see Fig. 7-24).

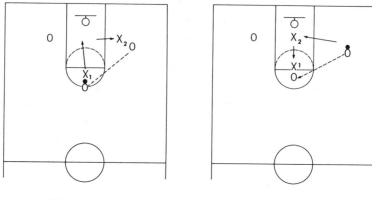

FIGURE 7-23   FIGURE 7-24

If a single player is caught in a two-on-one situation, she must retreat to the middle of the lane and attempt to keep the offensive players off balance by feinting. Her objective must be to slow down the offense until help arrives. However, as both players close in on the goal, she inevitably must commit herself to defend against the player with the ball. Although this leaves an opponent open for a possible pass, such a pass *must be made successfully* before it can hurt. Many bad passes are thrown while a player is traveling at full speed and many poorly thrown passes are fumbled. Remember: *Only the player with the ball can score.*

FULL COURT PRESSURE DEFENSES

The full court pressing defenses have gained widespread popularity among the top men's teams in the country. These defenses, if executed properly, should be even more effective in women's basketball. Many women's teams have only one or two polished ball handlers, thus making the team very vulnerable to a pressure defense.

Man-to-Man Press

The man-to-man press is a very demanding press in which each player must be able to match the skill and ability of the opponent she is guarding. After a score, as the ball comes through the net each defensive player must quickly locate her defensive responsibility. The player guarding the throw-in should overplay to either the right or left, forcing the offensive team to go only one way with the ball. This allows the defensive team to cover the most likely areas in which the ball will enter the court (see Fig. 7-25).

As in the straight man-to-man defense, the players away from the ball play their defensive opponents loosely. In this type of defense, the defensive players must either cut-off the passing lanes to the players they are guarding, or must try to herd their opponents into a double-team situation on the throw-in (see Fig. 7-26).

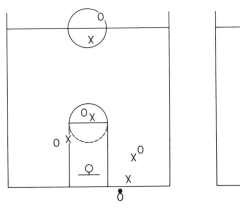

FIGURE 7-25

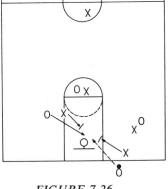

FIGURE 7-26

The smart coach will alternate the defensive emphasis on the man-to-man press. According to a pre-conceived pattern, or on a signal, the defense should either cut off the passing lanes or try to force the offensive players toward the ball for the quick double-team situation on the throw-in. The offensive team is *most vulnerable* to the man-to-man press *on the throw-in*.

If the throw-in is successful and the offensive team begins to advance the ball, the defense should apply the following general principles:

1. The player who receives the throw-in should not be allowed to pass the ball to the outside along the side lines. An attempt should be made to divert all passing toward the middle of the court. This is the area of congestion where space is limited and defensive help may be gained.
2. The offensive player must be kept from dribbling the ball up the floor. The dribbler should be forced toward the outside to use the side line for a trapping situation. This dribbler must not be allowed to dribble past the defensive player along the sideline. She must be harrassed and forced to pick up the dribble.

3. All players on the same side of the court as the ball should be over-played.

4. Any time the ball is passed, the defensive player should release and attempt an interception.

1-3-1 Zone Press

The 1-3-1 zone press employs the double team concept after the throw-in. The throw-in is not contested, but a double team is effected by the point player and the wing player on the same side as the ball. The middle player in the 1-3-1 is responsible for the pass down the sidelines and the wing player away from the ball shifts either forward or backward to overplay the area in which the pass is most likely to be attempted (see Fig. 7-27).

The players putting on the double team attempt to make the offensive player throw a high, lobbing pass which may be intercepted.

If the ball is passed to the opposite side of the floor, the wing player on that side attempts an interception or maintains a good defensive position in preparation for the double team, according to her position on the floor at the time of the pass. The point player moves to effect the double team (see Fig. 7-28).

Once it is evident that the offensive team has penetrated the zone press, it is essential that the defense immediately drops into its regular defensive pattern to prevent a delayed fast break situation.

2-2-1 Zone Press

In employing the 2-2-1 zone press, the defensive team allows the offense to inbound the ball, but must limit the throw-in to the area in front of the defense and *never* behind the front line of the defense.

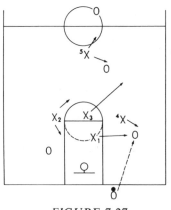

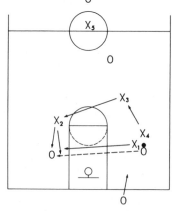

FIGURE 7-27   FIGURE 7-28

After the ball is in play, the front defensive player on the side of the ball moves to guard the player with the ball, making sure to keep her from dribbling up the sideline. The other front defensive player will defend the middle to stop the return pass to the player making the throw-in, or to a player cutting in the vicinity of the free throw lane. The defensive player in the second line on the same side as the ball, moves to the sideline to protect against the possible pass along the sideline. The second line player away from the ball moves toward the top of the key in a position to intercept any attempted cross-court pass. The back, or safety, player moves toward the ball side of the court and should go after any long pass that is thrown (see Fig. 7-29).

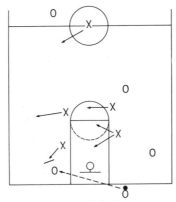

FIGURE 7-29

In all pressure defenses chances must be taken. An effective press is predicated upon initiative and daring. The offensive team will break the press at times, but the hindrance and psychological stress on the team with the ball caused by an effective press, will more than balance the occasional easy basket by the offense.

CHAPTER VIII

TEAM DEFENSE FOR THE TWO-COURT GAME

MAN-TO-MAN DEFENSE

No matter what defensive alignment a team may usually employ, the man-to-man defense is the basic standard formation, and all teams must be able to use it effectively. This implies that not only must each member of the team be skillful in executing the individual defensive fundamentals, but that each must also understand the team play element of the man-to-man concept.

The basic principle of this defense is that the players nearest the ball should always be putting pressure on their respective offensive opponents, and the players away from the ball should be sagging (see Fig. 8-1).

This concept is fundamental. With novice teams it is quite common to see a free offensive player (O_2) lose her guard (X_2) and drive right by another defensive player (X_1) who is unaware that she is in a position

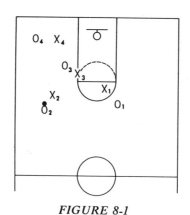

FIGURE 8-1

142

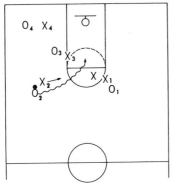
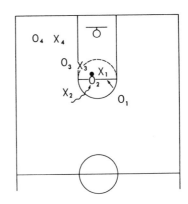

FIGURE 8-2   FIGURE 8-3

to help (see Fig. 8-2). In this situation, if X_1 had been sagging, she could have picked up the driving player and probably would have discouraged the offensive player from attempting the tactic in the first place (see Fig. 8-3).

When a guard loses her offensive opponent as X_2 did in the above situation, she should immediately drop back to the middle of the lane and pick up the player who is loose as the result of the switch made by X_1 (see Fig. 8-4).

Both X_3 and X_4 must be alert for a possible pass to the forwards they are guarding. In the front court near the goal, however, the person with the ball is the focal point of defensive strategy and she must be stopped before defensive players begin worrying about a possible pass-off. Remember: *only the player with the ball can score!* There is no advan-

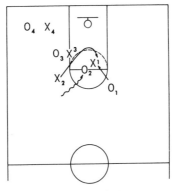

FIGURE 8-4

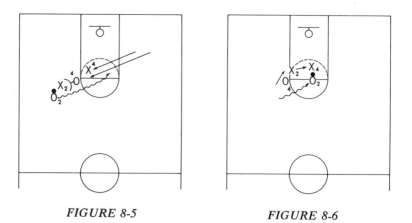

FIGURE 8-5   FIGURE 8-6

tage in having all of the potential passes defensed if the person with the ball is allowed to shoot and scores. Whenever a decision must be made regarding which player to cover, the defense must go after the person with the ball even though it means leaving a potential scorer open.

Almost all teams employ screening tactics against a man-to-man defense. Whenever a defensive player is screened, the closest teammate should call out "switch" if it is clear that the blocked player cannot slide through the screen. The player calling the switch picks up the offensive player of the girl who was screened, and the screened guard covers the offensive opponent of the girl who called the switch (see Figs. 8-5 and 8-6).

When offensive players cross-over, the defensive player (X_2) guarding the girl with the ball should, if possible, slide through between the other

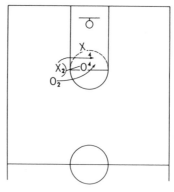

FIGURE 8-7

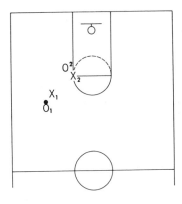

FIGURE 8-8

defensive player (X_4) and the person she is guarding (O_4) (see Fig. 8-7). She should never cross behind her teammate as this sets up a perfect screen and frees her opponent for an unguarded set shot.

The experienced offensive player will attempt to feint her opponent into defensive errors and guarding players must learn not to overreact to such maneuvers. Right handed players usually prefer to dribble and drive to the right, and defensive players should overplay an opponent with this tendency forcing her to drive only to her left.

Defending the Post Player

A high-scoring pivot player who gets the ball in or around the lane will usually score or draw a foul, so the ball must be kept from her as

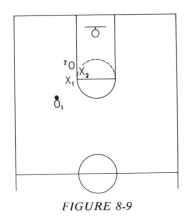

FIGURE 8-9

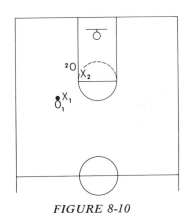

FIGURE 8-10

much as possible. The defensive player guarding the post player should position herself between the post and the ball to the extent that she can do so without giving her opponent an untenable advantage on a possible break toward the goal (see Fig. 8-8). The relative difference in playing ability between the two opponents determines how much risk X_2 can afford to take in keeping between the post player and the ball.

Any player guarding an opponent with the ball must decide how closely to play her defense. In general: (1) if the opposing player is a poor shot, she should sag making it difficult for her opponent to get the ball in to the pivot player (see Fig. 8-9);   or   (2) if the opponent is a good shot, she should play her tightly attempting to force a hurried and perhaps poorly thrown pass to the post (see Fig. 8-10).

To assist the player guarding the pivot, a defensive player in the area behind the post position should sag to cover the possibility of a high lob pass to the post player behind her guard (see Fig 8-11).

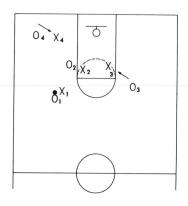

FIGURE 8-11

ZONE DEFENSE

The effective zone defense requires quick, alert players who refuse to give up. Although it is a physically demanding defense, it is the strongest rebounding formation that a team can use and is a style of play which can demoralize an offensive team not having an exceptional shooting night from the field.

Zone defenses are ball-oriented, as man-to-man is player-oriented. This means that each defensive player should be facing the ball at all times — a position which permits easy lateral movements as well as forward and backward moves. Each member of the zone should keep her hands up, maintain a continual chatter with her teammates, and *always* keep her feet pointed toward the ball.

The Box (2-2) Zone Defense

The box zone is really a disguised diamond defense. Although it starts out as a 2-2 pattern (see Fig. 8-12), a transition is made as soon as the ball is passed to a side position and it quickly becomes a 1-2-1 defense. As the ball moves to the side, player X_2 becomes the point of the defense and player X_4 shifts across the lane on the side of the ball. Player X_3 shifts to the middle of the lane, and player X_1 drops into the top of the free-throw circle (see Fig. 8-13).

The diamond-shaped defense is now revealed. As the ball moves into the corner, player X_4 moves to the corner to challenge the ball, player X_3 moves completely across the lane, player X_2 moves slightly back now that she is not guarding the ball, and player X_1 drops completely back to cover the long pass across the lane and to rebound the opposite side of the goal (see Fig. 8-14).

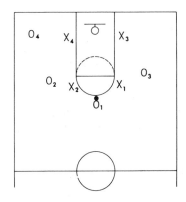

FIGURE 8-12

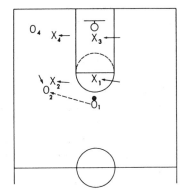

FIGURE 8-13

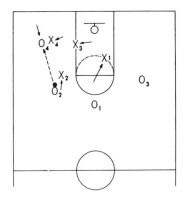

FIGURE 8-14

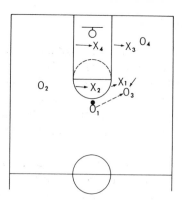

FIGURE 8-15

As the ball moves to the opposite side of the floor, the procedure is reversed. Player X_1 becomes the point of the defense, player X_3 shifts across the lane on the side of the ball, player X_4 Shifts to the middle of the lane, and player X_2 drops into the top of the free throw circle (see Fig. 8-15).

As the ball moves into the corner, player X_3 moves to the corner, player X_4 moves completely across the lane, player X_1 drops back now that the ball has left her zone, and player X_2 drops completely back to cover the long pass across the lane and to become the rebounder on the opposite side of the goal (see Fig. 8-16).

The back players must always shift completely across the lane when the ball moves to the corners. This necessary maneuver leaves the zone

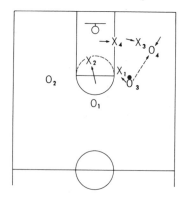

FIGURE 8-16

vulnerable to a cross-court pass beneath the goal, but this is an almost impossible pass to complete against an alert defensive team.

A zone defense is always weak against a team that moves the ball quickly and employs good fakes. Therefore, the zone must be given the illusion of solidarity. This can be accomplished by always having the players' hands outstretched. This simple fundamental makes the zone look tough in areas where it actually is very weak.

Talking on defense cannot be overemphasized. It is a simple fact that an offensive team can be discouraged from taking advantage of an opening by an alert defensive team shouting, "watch the cutter," or "watch the pass to the pivot player."

Midcourt Zone (Zone Press)

A midcourt defensive alignment can put a great deal of pressure on the offensive team by not allowing them to advance the ball easily into the scoring area. It also provides the defensive team with opportunities to make the offensive team commit errors which may result in a turnover of the ball.

The purpose of a zone press in girl's basketball is to make the offensive team throw long, high trajectory passes. The defensive team must play aggressively and be willing to take chances to intercept these throws.

The standard midcourt defensive alignment will have two stationary offensive players and a rover on the front line, one stationary defensive player and one rover on the second line, and a stationary defensive player at the back of the defense (see Fig. 8-17).

As the ball advances up the floor, the defensive player nearest the ball stops the dribble. This defensive player must always be sure to turn the

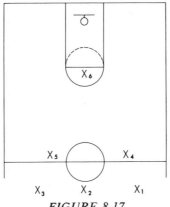

FIGURE 8-17

dribbler inside. If the dribbler gets by the first defensive player in the side lines, the defense is penetrated and becomes useless.

With the ball on the right side of the floor, player X_1 challenges the dribbler, player X_2 drops slightly back toward the center, player X_4

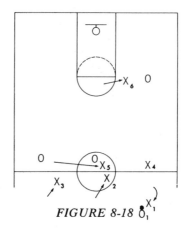

FIGURE 8-18

moves up to the center line on the same side as the ball, player X_5 moves to the center circle, and player X_6 moves toward the right side-line (see Fig. 8-18).

If the ball is passed back to the center, the mid-court zone shifts back to its original position. If the ball is passed to the left, player X_3 challenges the ball (not letting the girl with the ball dribble to the outside), player X_2 drops slightly back toward the center, player X_1 drops back and toward the center, player X_5 moves up to the center line on the same side as the ball, player X_4 moves to the center circle, and player X_6 moves toward the left sidelines (see Fig. 8-19).

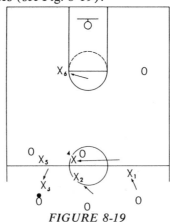

FIGURE 8-19

Any player on the second line can cross the center line to intercept a pass. If the person on the front line furthest from the ball, either player X_2 or X_3, drops back across the center line, both of the second line players can come across the center line to intercept passes.

The success of the midcourt zone will depend upon the defense always stopping the dribbler, always anticipating the obvious pass, and always going after the ball aggressively whenever it is in the air.

Once the ball crosses the center line, the defensive players drop back into their regular positions immediately. The second line player on the side opposite the side where the ball crosses over, must immediately get back to help the back defensive player forestall a two-on-one situation (see Fig. 8-20).

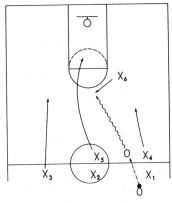

FIGURE 8-20

As in any zone defense, the defensive players must talk to each other and attempt to give the impression that the defense is stronger than it is. The defensive team must acknowledge the fact that a good offensive team is going to penetrate the zone and score at times, but the goal of the zone defense is to keep these penetrations at a minimum, and to force the offense to shoot from the outside as often as possible.

CHAPTER IX

COACHING PROBLEMS

An essential start on the road to success as a basketball coach is a thorough understanding of conditioning theory and the related practical techniques for developing a high level of physical and mental fitness in athletes. Of parallel importance are a broad knowledge of the basic fundamentals of the game and the ability to teach these movements both as individual skills and as the complex coordinations which make up the various patterns of offensive and defensive team play. Finally, each of these specific competencies must be tied together through a sound grasp of game tactics and strategy. The degree to which a coach gets this overall job done correlates highly with the achievement of a winning season.

Unfortunately, however, most of the factors involved in this process are not clear-cut. There are myriad details along each step of the road and the successful coach, like any good administrator, must deal with these various aspects of team management in an organized manner. Careful preparation must go into the planning for a basketball season and a great deal of the direction of this effort must be based upon the experience of the coach. No step-by-step listing of procedures leading to a successful season can be provided in a coaching text, and this is exactly why experience is invaluable in coaching athletics. Experience provides the coach with the knowledge of what "works" with her in the interpersonal relationships with the girls making up her squad. These techniques differ with every personality, and every novice coach has some trial-and-error learning to muddle through before she learns her trade.

There are broad guidelines, though, which will help any beginning coach with some of the mechanical problems which she inevitably will face, and the purpose of this chapter is to suggest general solutions to some of these situations.

PRE-SEASON PROBLEMS

Scheduling

Whenever possible, scheduling should be completed well in advance of the first practice session. If the team is a member of a conference, all league games must, of course, be scheduled first. After the conference schedule is completed, open dates can be filled in with non-conference opponents. An important consideration in scheduling is to arrange road games in such a manner that the players will miss a minimum of class or work time. In general, it is wise to schedule away games on weekends. Coaches should avoid the "prestige schedule" trap which usually calls for extensive, tiring trips and which is subject to the additional built-in disadvantage of playing on someone else's home courts. Ths situation, obviously, is not conducive to a favorable win-loss record. Schedule makers should try to include all of the good teams in the home area before being too concerned about getting distant good teams on the agenda.

Uniforms

Uniforms can be of great psychological advantage to the team that is attractively attired. Being smartly dressed is a potent morale factor which is reflected in a team's attitude and play. Proper fit should be insisted upon by the coach. Uniforms should be fitted shortly after the first practice and the need for alterations should be noted and attended to immediately.

The conscientious coach will insist that all uniforms be worn in the same manner. It is wise to let the team members decide on such details as how to wear their socks or whether to wear their jackets buttoned or unbuttoned. After these decisions are made, however, it should be understood that all team members will follow the desires of the majority.

Many teams wear a distinctive traveling uniform. Most often this consists of a blazer and skirt, although sometimes a sweater and skirt or an attractively styled dress, are selected. With many teams each player is responsible for purchasing her own travel uniform. Perhaps the least expensive way of obtaining traveling uniforms is to arrange to have such costumes made by a local seamstress at the expense of the players. Under no circumstances should players be allowed to travel in slacks, shorts, or other inappropriate dress.

154   COACHING PROBLEMS

FIGURE 9-1   Sample Player Information Form

Student Number_____
WOMEN'S BASKETBALL INFORMATION SHEET
Midwestern College
Please Print   Year — 19____
Name_____/_____/_____
            (Last)   (First)   (Middle Initial)
Street address_____
Hometown & state_____
High school attended_____
Month & year graduated from high school_____
If transfer student — indicate college attended_____
                — indicate semesters attended_____
                — indicate month & year left that college_____
Parents' names — Father_____Mother_____
or name of guardian — Mr. or Mrs._____
Street address of parents or guardian_____
Hometown & state of parents or guardian_____
Parents or guardian home phone number — area code____phone no.____
Hometown paper & address (city & state)_____
Age_____   Position played in H.S._____
Height_____   Position played in college_____
Shoe size_____   Position you would like to play
        Low cut or high top   at Midwestern_____
                            Scoring average in H.S._____
                            Rebounding average_____
                            Number of assists per game_____
Number of years played basketball in high school_____
Years lettered in high school basketball_____
Honors won playing basketball in high school—(captain, MVP, state honors, records, etc.) _____

Year at Midwestern College (Please circle one)   Freshman   Sophomore
                                        Junior   Senior
Semester at Midwestern College (Please circle one) 1 2 3 4 5 6 7 8 9 10
Number of years played basketball at Midwestern College_____
Single or married?_____If married, how many children?_____
Name of your husband (First name)_____Names of your children

Married how many years?_____Church Preference_____
Place of residence at Midwestern (Building)_____(Room no.)____
Address in Denison if living off campus_____
Telephone number_____
Major field in college_____Minor_____
Basketball coach in high school_____

FIGURE 9-2   Sample Class Schedule Form

CLASS SCHEDULE
Midwestern College

Name_____ Trimester & Year_____

Student's Number_____ Telephone Number_____

Place of residence on campus_____

         (Housing Unit)   (Room Number)

Time	Monday	Tuesday	Wednesday	Thursday	Friday	Saturday
8:00						
9:00						
10:00						
11:00						
12:00						
1:00						
2:00						
3:00						
4:00						
5:00						
Night						

	Credit		
Courses Scheduled	*Hours*	*Building & Room*	*Instructor*

The team should be provided with practice uniforms, socks, shoes, and towels for each training session and the laundering of these items should be handled by the school or club.

Preliminary Team Meeting

At the first meeting of the candidates for the squad, the responsibilities of the player to the coach, the coach to the player, and of both to the school or club, must be discussed thoroughly. A player questionnaire providing various information needed by the coach (see Fig. 9-1) and a class schedule (see Fig. 9-2) should be completed by each athlete. Typical of the items which might be considered at this meeting are the following which normally are included on the agenda of the initial turn-out meeting at Midwestern College.

1. Completion of player questionnaire forms.
2. Completion of player class schedules.
3. Dissemination of practice schedule.
4. Dissemination of game schedule.
5. Discussion of eligibility rules.
6. Discussion of medical examination policy.
7. Discussion of team insurance program.
8. Discussion of procedures for extra-school visits to the doctor or dentist.
9. Discussion of the coach's method of choosing the team.
10. Discussion of equipment provided by the school or club.
11. Discussion of equipment to be provided by individual team members.
12. Discussion of travel, policies and procedures.
13. Discussion of training rules.
14. Discussion of the objectives of the team for the season.

PRACTICE SEASON PROBLEMS

Injuries

It is the responsibility of the trainer to maintain a running list of all injuries, the treatment of these injuries, and the progress of the injuries. On many teams the coach must also double as the trainer. If this is the case, the coach must train the team manager in basic training room procedures and first aid techniques. Most of the routine injuries can be cared for by the manager. All unusual or serious problems should be cared for by the head trainer, the coach, or a physician. It is especially important that post-injury treatment be checked by the coach. Players are notorious for their lack of judgment in caring for themselves during recuperative periods.

Team Practice

It is essential that the coach have a practice plan for the entire season. Every phase of the game must be covered in a sequential pattern, and many coaches find it helpful to use a checklist to insure that each is provided for. The following listing indicates the items which are included on such a checklist at Midwestern College:

Special Conditioning
_____ Circuit training
_____ Weight training

Individual Defense
_____ Defensive drills
_____ Blocking out and rebounding
_____ Recovering drills
_____ Loose ball drills

Individual Offense
_____ Shooting drills
_____ Rebounding drills
_____ Pivoting drills
_____ Passing drills
_____ Dribbling drills
_____ Ball handling drills
_____ Faking drills

Team Defense
_____ Man-to-man defense
_____ Zone defense
Full court pressure defenses
_____ a. Zone
_____ b. Man-to-man
_____ c. Combination
_____ Stall defense

Team Offense
_____ Fast break drills
_____ Offense against man-to-man defense
_____ Offense against zone defense
_____ Ball control offense
_____ Out of bounds plays

Special situations
Free throw alignments
_____ a. Offense
_____ b. Defense
Jump balls
_____ a. Offense
_____ b. Defense

Many experienced coaches make out weekly practice plans as an aid in keeping objectives for each week in mind. Daily practice plans based on such a week's schedule and providing a time allotment for each item on the agenda, should be written out prior to each session. Maintaining a precise time schedule is of the utmost importance. On some occasions, no matter how much time is spent on a specific outcome, the desired level of achievement will not be realized on that particular day. In such situations the use of a daily plan will aid the coach in keeping the practice session on the predetermined time schedule thus avoiding an untenable shortchanging of other essential aspects of the planned practice. There is no leeway in a normal season for an inefficient use of time on the practice court.

Following are actual daily practice plans for a typical week at Midwestern College:

Midwestern College Weekly Practice Schedule

MONDAY

Pre-practice	Circuit training
6:00 – 6:20 p.m.	Free and spot shooting
6:20 – 6:30 p.m.	Combination drill
6:30 – 6:40 p.m.	Free throw drill
6:40 – 7:10 p.m.	Specific individual defensive technique drills
7:10 – 7:20 p.m.	Specific individual offensive technique drills
7:20 – 7:30 p.m.	Defensive conditioning drills
7:30 – 7:45 p.m.	Team defense
7:45 – 7:55 p.m.	Combination drill
7:55 – 8:00 p.m.	Verbal review and forecast

TUESDAY

Pre-practice	Circuit training
6:00 – 6:20 p.m.	Free and spot shooting
6:20 – 6:30 p.m.	Combination drill
6:30 – 6:45 p.m.	Defensive rebounding drill
6:45 – 7:00 p.m.	Dummy offense
7:00 – 7:15 p.m.	Half court offense vs. defense
7:15 – 7:35 p.m.	Pressure defense — full court
7:35 – 7:45 p.m.	Free throw drill
7:45 – 7:55 p.m.	Team defense — half court

WEDNESDAY

Pre-practice	Circuit training
6:00 – 6:20 p.m.	Free and spot shooting
6:20 – 6:30 p.m.	Combination drill
6:30 – 6:50 p.m.	Team defense
6:50 – 7:10 p.m.	Dummy offense

7:10 – 7:30 p.m.   Fast break drill
7:30 – 7:50 p.m.   Full court scrimmage
7:50 – 8:00 p.m.   Verbal review and forecast

THURSDAY

Pre-practice   Circuit training
6:00 – 6:10 p.m.   Offensive rebounding drill
6:10 – 6:20 p.m.   Jump ball situations
6:20 – 6:50 p.m.   Free shooting
6:50 – 7:00 p.m.   Out of bounds defense
7:00 – 7:10 p.m.   Out of bounds offense
7:10 – 7:30 p.m.   Pressure defense — full court
7:30 – 7:45 p.m.   Combination fast break and fast break defense drills
7:45 – 7:55 p.m.   Pre-game warm up drill practice
7:55 – 8:00 p.m.   Verbal review and forecast

FRIDAY

Pre-practice   Circuit training
6:00 – 6:10 p.m.   Combination drill
6:10 – 6:20 p.m.   Defensive conditioning drill
6:20 – 6:40 p.m.   Team defense
6:40 – 6:55 p.m.   Dummy offense
6:55 – 7:10 p.m.   Pressure defense — full court
7:10 – 7:15 p.m.   30-second ball control
7:15 – 7:20 p.m.   30-second defense
7:20 – 7:45 p.m.   Full court scrimmage
7:45 – 7:50 p.m.   Free throw drill
7:50 – 7:55 p.m.   Verbal review and forecast

Switching Positions

In connection with the two-court game, a common coaching error to be avoided is that of working players in only one position. The entire team will function more efficiently as a unit if the guards learn to play offensive positions and the forwards learn the specific defensive tactics of the guards. The wise coach will allow the guards to switch positions with the forwards in practice and easy games. Utilizing this method, a respect for the other person's task is developed and the emergency situation in which a key player must play out of her normal position is provided for.

Attitude Toward Practice

All games are won or lost on the practice floor. The coach should emphasize constantly the fact that athletes play the game exactly as they practice. Often teams are concerned about being "up" for a specific game. As important as psychological preparation is, however, it can only help if the ground work of fundamental individual and team skills is properly laid in practice.

PLAYING SEASON PROBLEMS

Scouting

A scouting report is always a valuable asset in the preparation of a team for its next game. Probably the coach can never have enough data on the opposing teams on the schedule. Individual players, however, can have too much information. A surplus of scouting material given to the team prior to each game can be confusing.

Several athletic equipment manufacturing companies publish effective forms for use in scouting opposing teams, but most coaches prepare their own data gathering forms. Items of specific interest which should be included in any scouting report include:

1. Analyses of the basic offenses.
2. Analyses of the basic defenses.
3. Team characteristics (size, speed, physical condition).
4. Individual characteristics (player idiosyncracies).
5. Rebounding effectiveness.
6. Out of bounds plays.
7. Jump ball line-up and/or plays .
8. Offense in pressure situations.
9. Who gets the ball when two points are needed?

Special Preparation

There is an old coaching adage that states, "Play your own game." This is valid advice. Acknowledging the necessity of making a major change to combat the strengths of an opponent is an admission of weakness which can be psychologically defeating. If at all possible, necessary adjustments should be kept to a minimum. A team should concentrate on developing its offenses and defenses to a degree of efficiency that causes the opponents to make the major adjustments.

Psychological Preparation

Psychological preparation for specific games should not be under-rated. A coach basing her philosophy of coaching on the concept implied in the statement, "Preparation coupled with inspiration equals victory," has the proper understanding of what it takes to be a winning coach.

Among some of the more widely used methods of getting a team "up" for a game are:

1. Slogans, signs, and newspaper clippings in the locker room and gymnasium.
2. Pep rallies.
3. Wearing distinctive clothes on the day of the game.
4. Fast and catchy music played in the dressing room.
5. Pre-game pep talks by the coach.
6. Silence observed in the locker room before the game.
7. Inspirational music in the locker room.
8. Viewing inspirational movies.
9. Taping the reading of an inspirational poem with appropriate background music.

All of these techniques can produce results. A coach must know her team to be able to gauge which technique or combination of techniques will prove effective.

Warm Up Drills

Many coaches believe that pre-game warm up drills should be based upon patterns which will be used by the team in its various offenses during the game. Other coaches are of the opinion that such drills should be psychologically appealing to both the players and the fans. At Midwestern College it is believed that the pre-game routine should warm up the players physiologically and also provide a psychological lift. The rationale is that if previous preparation has been adequate, it should not be necessary to review offensive and defensive play as part of the pre-game routine.

Times-Out

The coach should call *all* times-out. This axiom is especially valid when coaching a young and relatively inexperienced team. If the coach has a great deal of confidence in her floor captain she may allow her to assume this responsibility, but the indiscriminate calling of time by any player cannot be allowed.

Changing Rovers

In the two-court game, coaches have two options concerning the resting of their rovers: (1) the coach can substitute for the rover; or (2) the players can switch positions on their own volition. At Midwestern College it was believed that the second alternative is the best choice. Actually, the goal of all coaches should be to put six players on the floor who can rove.

Substitutions

The coach must develop an intimate knowledge of her players and their capabilities, both psychologically and physically. A player who is not having a good night should be taken out of the game. Too often a coach will keep a star player in the game even when her poor excution is obviously hurting the overall team performance. The coach must have the courage to make needed adjustments in her line up. Incidentally, many times a brief stint on the bench will help alleviate the complacency of a star player.

Statistics

Statistics must be kept for each game and these data must be cumulative for the entire season. The coach should be able to check the statistical situation as it relates to the team and to the individual players at any point in the season. Since statistical records are no better than the original data from which they are derived, it is very important that a team manager or a team assistant be carefully trained in the collecting of such information.

Each coach will have her own ideas relating to the nature of the statistics to be gathered, but one essential is to keep a chart of shots attempted and made (see Fig. 9-3). Most coaches feel that it is also important to keep a record of rebounds, assists, stolen balls, and turn-overs. A statistical overview of both teams should be compiled from the shot chart and the score book (see Fig. 9-4) after each game. A cumulative record should be maintained on each player as well as on the team as a whole (see Fig. 9-5).

The coach should avoid letting statistics control her attitudes concerning individual players. A poor average shooter (one whose statistical shooting average is poor) may always do her best against strong competition. The poor average foul shooter may always come through when the pressure is on. Sometimes a leading scorer seldom has a good night against top competition. Raw statistics can be very misleading. They must be interpreted intelligently.

Films and Video Tapes

A visual play-back of action involving errors (or correct execution) is normally an excellent teaching aid and most coaches find the use of

Date_____Place_____Game No._____

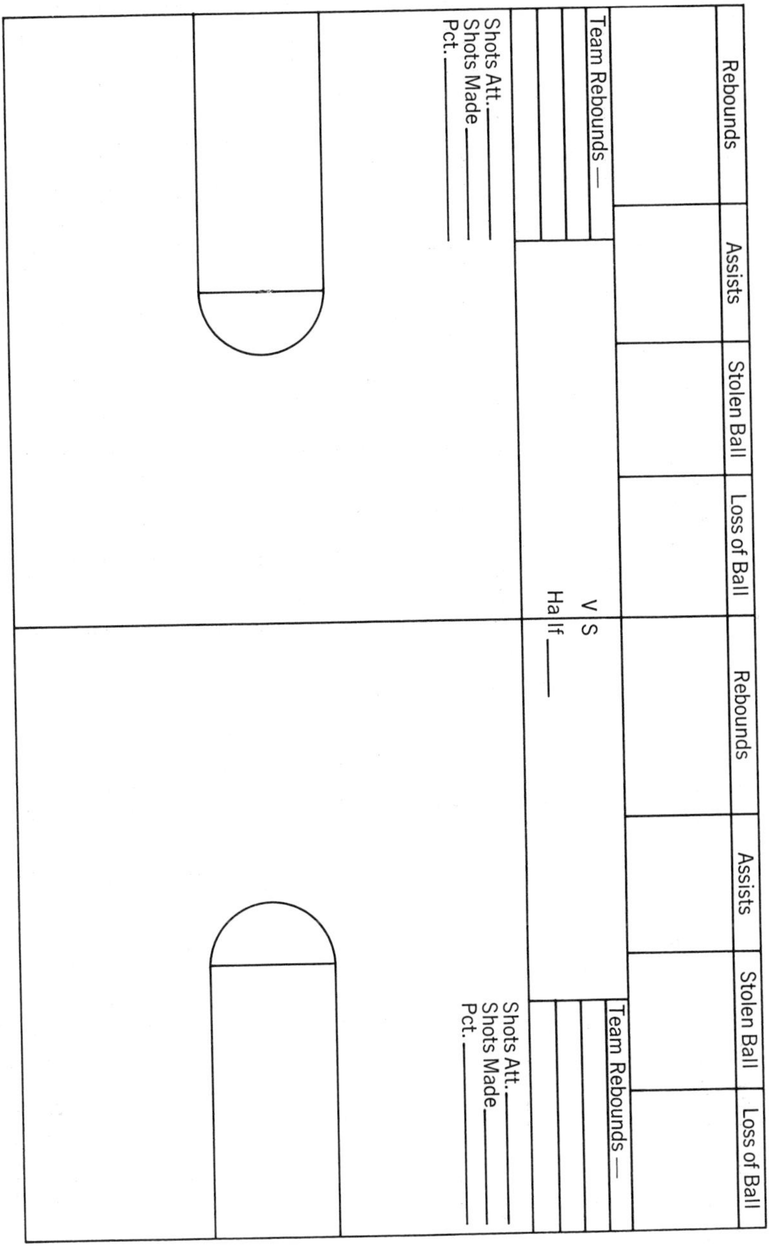

Rebounds	Assists	Stolen Ball	Loss of Ball	Rebounds	Assists	Stolen Ball	Loss of Ball

Team Rebounds —

Shots Att.——
Shots Made——
Pct.——

V S
Half ——

Team Rebounds —

Shots Att.——
Shots Made——
Pct.——

FIGURE 9-3   Sample Shot Chart

FIGURE 9-4   *Sample Statistical Overview*

Official Basketball Box _____ Date _____ Home _____ Away _____ Men _____ Women _____ JV _____

Midwestern College vs _____   Place _____

Game Totals   SCORE BY PERIODS

            1   2   3   4   EP   EP   EP   EP   Final

Record to date — Won _____ Lost _____

Team ( )	G	Field Goals			Free Throws			Rebounds		Fouls		Ast.	R	L	Points	Avg.
		Att.	Made	%	Att.	Made	%	No.	Avg.	No.	Disq.					
Midwestern Totals																
Opponent's Totals																

FIGURE 9-5 *Sample Cumulative Statistics Summary*

CUMULATIVE BASKETBALL STATISTICS SUMMARY
Midwestern College

Name _____

Number Games	Field Goals			Free Throws			Shots	Rebounds		Fouls		Points		Assists	
	Scored	Atts.	Pct.	Scored	Atts.	Pct.	Missed	No.	Avg.	No.	Disq.	No.	Avg.	(L)	(S)

films to be invaluable in teaching basketball skills. Even with a limited budget, coaches generally feel that it is a must to film two or three ball games per year. Actually, such coverage can be produced relatively inexpensively with 8 mm or Super 8mm film and equipment.

Many schools now own video tape recorders. When available, these machines should be used extensively to tape practice sessions. Such tapes can be erased and reused and will prove to be of tremendous help in any coaching/teaching situation.

Staleness

Many teams are plagued by middle or late season staleness. There are several techniques which may be utilized by the coach to forestall psychological let-downs among the members of her squad:

1. Set realistic team goals and review the current progress toward the goals at frequent intervals.
2. Add new drills periodically, or drills which involve fancy ball handling. With the new challenge, players often regain their enthusiasm.
3. Introduce fast and catchy recorded music in the practice sessions.
4. Give the team a day, or days, off from practice. Do not allow them to touch a basketball during this period.
5. Arrange a volleyball tournament at one or several successive practices.
6. Hold a new game or practice uniform in reserve. When staleness occurs, issue the new equipment.

POST-SEASON PROBLEMS

Naming a Captain

A captain for the succeeding year should be named at the conclusion of each season. Until a tradition of excellence has been established, the captain should be appointed by the coach. Once a winning tradition is on a solid base, however, the players will be able to elect a captain with the seriousness of purpose the job requires. A coach simply cannot allow a popularity contest to decide the team captain.

Inventory

Immediately after the close of the season, players should turn in *all* the equipment which has been issued to them. At this time the coach and manager should inventory the equipment. This inventory list should indicate the need for repair and replacement (see Fig. 9-6). All repairable items should be repaired immediately and stored. Do not give used equipment or uniforms to the players. Expendable items can be used in practice or can be given to other teams in need of such materials.

FIGURE 9-6   Sample Inventory Form

EQUIPMENT INVENTORY LIST
Midwestern College

Sport_____   Year_____

Item Description	Size	On Hand	New Items	Total Items	Non Usable	Needs Repair	Total Next S.

Budget

A realistic budget for the succeeding year should be prepared shortly after completion of each season. The budget should be based upon the current season's expenditures, the need for additional equipment and supplies, and any expansion to be made in the program. After the budget has been approved, the coach should maintain a weekly budget report indicating the amount of money expended and the amount remaining (see Fig. 9-7). Such a weekly review is a good business practice which will be appreciated by the school or club fiscal officer. It also is extremely helpful to the coach in avoiding inadvertent overspending of available resources.

FIGURE 9-7   Sample Weekly Budget Report Form

ATHLETIC BUDGET
Weekly Report
Midwestern College

Sport_____   Trimester & Year_____

Sports Area	Amount Allowed			Amount Used			Amount Received		Balance Left	
1. Travel										
2. Equipment										
3. Officials										
4. Filming										
5. Scouting										
6. Guarantees										
7. Recruiting & Coaching Clinics										
8. Repair										
9. Medical Expense										
10. Field & Gym Rental										
11. Awards										
12. General Expense										
13. Miscellaneous Expense										
Others										
Others										

Total Amount Allowed for Sport $_____

Total Amount Used to Date $_____

Balance Left $_____

Copies to:

_____

_____   Athletic Business Manager

_____

_____   _____

LIST OF ILLUSTRATIONS

BIBLIOGRAPHY

Anderson, Forrest and Stan Albeck, *Coaching Better Basketball.* New York: Ronal Press Co., 1964.

Baisi, Neal, *Coaching the Zone and Man-to-Man Pressing Defenses.* Englewood Cliffs, N. J.: Prentice-Hall, Inc., 1961.

Bee, Clair and Ken Norton, *Basketball Fundamentals and Techniques.* New York; Ronald Press Co., 1959

Bee, Clair and Ken Norton, *Basketball Man-to-Man Defense and Attack.* New York: Ronald Press Co., 1959.

Bee, Clair and Ken Norton, *Individual and Team Basketball Drills.* New York: Ronald Press Co., 1959.

Bee, Clair and Ken Norton, *The Science of Coaching Basketball.* New York: Ronald Press Co., 1959.

Bee, Clair, *Winning Basketball Plays.* New York: Ronald Press Co., 1963.

Bell, Mary M., *Women's Basketball.* Dubuque, Iowa: Wm. C. Brown Co., 1964.

Bunn, John, *The Basketball Coach: Guides to Success.* Englewood Cliffs, N. J., Prentice-Hall, Inc., 1961.

Bunn, John, *Basketball Techniques and Team Play.* Englewood Cliffs, N. J.: Prentice-Hall, Inc., 1964.

Cooper, John M. and Daryl Siedentop, *The Theory and Science of Basketball.* Philadelphia: Lea & Febiger, 1969.

Eaves, Joel, *Basketball's Shuffle Offense.* Englewood Cliffs ,N. J.: Prentice-Hall, Inc., 1961.

Gardner, Jack, *Championship Basketball With Jack Gardner.* Englewood Cliffs, N. J.: Prentice Hall, Inc., 1961.

Gill, A. T. "Slats", *Basic Basketball.* New York, Ronald Press Co., 1962.

Healey, William, *High School Basketball, Coaching, Managing, Administering.* Danville, Ill.: Interstate Printers and Publishers, Inc., 1962.

173

Jucker, Ed, *Cincinnati Power Basketball*. Englewood Cliffs, N. J.: Prentice-Hall, Inc., 1962.

LaGrand, Louis, *Coach's Complete Guide to Winning Basketball*. West Nyack, New York: Parker Publishing Co., 1967.

Lapchick, Joe and Clair Bee, *Fifty Years of Basketball*. Englewood Cliffs, N. J.: Prentice-Hall, Inc., 1968.

McGuire, Frank, *Team Basketball: Offense and Defense*. Englewood Cliffs, N. J.: Prentice-Hall, Inc., 1966.

Meyer, Ray, *Basketball as Coached by Ray Meyer*. Englewood Cliffs, N. J.: Prentice-Hall, Inc., 1967.

Neal, Patsy, *Basketball Techniques for Women*. New York: Ronald Press Co., 1966.

Newell, Pete and John Benington,, *Basketball Methods*. New York: Ronald Press Co., 1962.

Sports Illustrated Book of Basketball, Philadelphia: J. B. Lippincott Co., 1962.

Strack, David H., *Basketball*. Englewood Cliffs, N. J.: Prentice-Hall, Inc., 1968.

Teaque, Bertha Frank, *Basketball for Girls*. New York: Ronald Press, Co., 1962.

Wilkes, Glenn, *Basketball Coach's Complete Handbook*. Englewood Cliffs, N. J.: Prentice-Hall, Inc., 1962.

Wilkes, Glenn, *Winning Basketball Strategy*. Englewood Cliffs, N. J.: Prentice-Hall, Inc., 1959.

Winter, Tex, *The Triple-Post Offense*, Englewood Cliffs, N. J. Prentice-Hall, Inc., 1962.

Wooden, John R., *Practical Modern Basketball*. New York: Ronald Press Co., 1966.

INDEX

AAHPER, 11, 18
AAU, 10, 11, 12, 13, 15, 16, 19
AAU-DGWS controversy, 11-13
Aerobic metabolism, 28, 29
Agility, 22, 24
Ainsworth, Dorothy, 7
All America team, first, 10
Amateur Athletic Union,
   10, 11, 12, 13, 15, 16, 19
American Association for Health,
  Physical Education, and
  Recreation, 11, 18
Amino acids, 28
Anaerobic metabolism, 27-28
Atlanta Blues, 11
Attitude toward practice, 48, 159-60
Australia, basketball in, 8

Baer, Clara, 6
Banks, Alline:
  eleven-time All American, 11
  Hall of Fame selection, 16
Barham, Leota, 16
Barnard College, 7
Baseball pass, 51
Basic principles of attacking
  the zone, 84-85, 89, 110
Basketball:
  a girl's game, 7-9
  fundamental principles of, 2-3
  in Australia, 8
  in Brazil, 8
  in England, 8
  in Japan, 8

in New Zealand, 8
in the Philippine Islands, 8
Basketball sense, 71
"Baskets," 3
"Basquette," 6
Berenson, Senda:
  opinion of basketball, 9
  rules committee member, 7
  Smith College, early play at, 5
Blann, Loretta, 16
Blue Eye, Missouri,
  training camp, 16-17, 19
Boston Normal School
  of Gymnastics, 7
Bounce pass, one-handed, 53, 54
Bounce pass, two-handed, 51-53
Bowden, Pauline, 14
Box defense,
  134, 135, 136, 137, 147-49
Boxer's shuffle, 69, 72
Brazil:
  basketball in, 8
  Pan American Games, 1959, 15
  Pan American Games, 1963, 16
  World Championships,
  Women's, 1967, 18
Bryn Mawr College, 7
Budget:
  procedures, 168-69
  weekly report form, 169
Bulgaria:
  World Championships,
  Women's, 1964, 16

175

176